THE HIGHLAND RAILWAY

This entertaining and fully-documented account of the Highland Railway has been completely revised and up-dated by C. R. Clinker.

Despite limited resources the Highland occupied third place among the five fully-independent pre-1923 mainline railways of Scotland. Its popularity among those who love railways arose both from the scenic charm of its terrain, and also from the way in which the small company worked its traffic in the face of natural difficulties over routes which were largely single track.

The story of the growth of the railway is told in detail and train services, locomotives and steamships have their own chapters. A vivid chapter on problems of operation highlights such aspects as fighting the winter snowfalls and the remarkable burden of traffic the limited system had to carry during the First World War.

Placed against the background of the country it served this is a history to be enjoyed by those interested in the Highlands generally as well as by railway enthusiasts.

'Never a rich railway, it was never a bad one and was of the greatest value in both world wars.'

The Times Literary Supplement

The David & Charles Series

THE HIGHLAND RAILWAY

H. A. VALLANCE

Revised and brought up to date
by
C. R. Clinker

PAN BOOKS LTD : LONDON

First published in 1938.
Revised and extended editions published 1963 and 1969
by David & Charles (Publishers) Ltd.
This edition published 1972 by Pan Books Ltd,
33 Tothill Street, London, SW1.

ISBN 0 330 02720 4

Printed and bound in England by
Hazell Watson & Viney Ltd,
Aylesbury, Bucks

CONTENTS

LIST OF ILLUSTRATIONS

FOREWORD

THIS BOOK had its origin in a paper read to members of the Railway Club more than thirty years ago. The enthusiasm with which that necessarily brief account of one of the most remarkable and fascinating railways in Great Britain was received encouraged me to present the subject in greater detail, and the first edition of this history appeared in 1938. The library of the Railway Club proved a most valuable source of reference.

The text has now been revised in the light of additional information and corrections that have come to light in recent years, and has been brought up to date to mark the approaching centenary of the opening of the main line from Forres to Perth. My task was made the easier by having ready access to the records now in the Archivist's Department of the British Transport Commission, which were not generally available thirty years ago. I must express my appreciation of the excellent way in which this mass of diverse material has been catalogued and stored, and to the assistance that I have received from the staff of the department, both in London and in Edinburgh. I am also grateful to Mr M. D. Greville, whose painstaking researches have revealed additional information and corrected some errors.

My thanks are due to His Grace the Duke of Sutherland for permission to reproduce the ticket of the Duke of Sutherland's Railway, now in the museum at Dunrobin Castle. I am also indebted to the railway enthusiasts who have allowed tickets and photographs from their collections to be used as illustrations. The proprietors of *The Railway Magazine* have generously made available the colour blocks of this illustration, and other items from their files.

The Railway Club
320 High Holborn
London, WC1
December 1962

H.A.V.

THURSO
Hoy
Halkirk
Scotscalder
Georgemas
Bower
Watten
Wick
Bilbster
Altnabreac
Forsinard
Thrumster
Ulbster
Mid-Clyth
Occumster
Lybster

Kinbrace
Borrobol
Platform
Kildonan
Salzcraggie
Platform
Helmsdale
Loth
Brora

L. SHIN

Lairg
Rogart
The
Mound
Dunrobin (Private)
Invershin
Culrain
Cambusavie
Platform
Golspie
Skelbo
Embo
DORNOCH
TAIN
Bonar
Bridge
Edderton
Fearn
Kildary
Nigg
Alness Delny
Foulis
Novar
Invergordon
Hopeman
Burghead
Lossiemouth
Portessie
Buckie
Rathven
L. FANNICH
Loch
Luichart
Achanalt
Achnasheen
Glencarron
Platform
Garve
Strathpeffer
DINGWALL
Fortrose
Fort George
NAIRN
Dalvey
Forres
Dunphail
Dava
Craigellachie
Orbliston
Orton
Elgin
Drybridge
Aultmore
KEITH
Achnashellach
Strathcarron
Attadale
Strome Ferry
Duirinish
KYLE OF
LOCHALSH
Plockton
Conon
Muir of Ord
Beauly
Clunes
Lentran
Redcastle
Allangrange
Munlochy
Avoch
Culloden Moor
Bunchrew
INVERNESS
Dalcross
Allanfearn
Dunphail
L. LUICHART
ISLE OF
SKYE
L. ALSH
Daviot
Moy
Tomatin
Grentown on Spey
SLOCHD
SUMMIT
Broomhill
Boat of Garten
AVIEMORE
L. NESS
Fort
Augustus
Carr
Bridge
L. LOICH
L. ARKAIG
L. LOCHY
Kincraig
Kingussie
Newtonmore
L. MORAR
Mallaig
Delwhinnie
DRUMUACHDAR
SUMMIT
Dalnaspidal
L. EIL
L. SHIEL
Fort
William
L. ERICHT
Blair
Atholl
Struan
Killiecrankie
Pitlochry
Kirriemuir
FORFAR
Ballachulish
L. RANNOCH
Grandfully
Aberfeldy
Ballinluig
Guay
Blairgowrie
Murthly
Alyth
L. LINNHE
L. ETIVE
Loch
Tay
L. TAY
Dalguise
Dunkeld
Balnacco
Methven
Stanley
Strathord
Luncarty
DUNDEE
OBAN
Crianlarich
Killin Jcn.
L. EARN
Crieff
PERTH
R. TAY

Map of the Highland Railway

INTRODUCTION TO THIS EDITION

STRANGE AS it may seem, only two of the five major pre-grouping railway companies in Scotland, the Highland and Great North of Scotland, have so far received anything approaching adequate historical treatment. Although their locomotives have been well written up, no definitive general histories of the Caledonian, Glasgow & South Western and North British companies have yet appeared.

The history of individual railways has so often been written, and quite satisfactorily so, by authors not native to the area concerned. It may, therefore, come as a surprise that Hugh Aymer Vallance was of Scottish ancestry and so felt at home in the district served by the Highland Railway. The first edition of his book, published in 1938, broke new ground, for it was in fact the first full-scale history of a Scottish railway company. A second, revised and extended edition appeared in 1963. In the present edition the original work has again been revised, slightly re-arranged and new material inserted to record in detail the widespread changes brought about by rationalization since 1960. Vallance's other books were *The Great North of Scotland Railway* and one on travel in Scandinavia. It was Vallance's belief that his readers were interested more in the history of the railways and less in their economic and social background; his books treat the subject accordingly, and the changes made in this edition respect his views.

In addition to his personal enthusiasm for railways, Vallance had practical experience of them on the engineering side and was widely known as a writer and lecturer. His 17-year association with *The Railway Magazine*, latterly as deputy-editor, brought him into contact by correspondence with a large number of people who shared his interests. Many will recall the help they received from him and the trouble he took in answering their letters.

If the name of MacDermot is inevitably associated with the Great Western, Grinling with the Great Northern and Tomlinson with the North Eastern, then so will Vallance be remembered as the historian of the Highland Railway.

C.R.C.

Padstow,
Cornwall.
July 1971

CHAPTER ONE

A FIGHT FOR A RAILWAY

FIRST MOVES

IN THE years following the Industrial Revolution, when many parts of the country were experiencing a trade boom, with its consequent increase of wealth, the Highlands of Scotland were plunged in the depths of financial depression, and poverty was rife. It was an era of great changes. The old clan system had been completely shattered by the Rebellion of 1745; and the landowners were turning their attention to sheep-farming on a large scale. Many of their tenants were compulsorily evicted from their homes, and forced to emigrate overseas, or to make their way to the cities in search of a livelihood.

The absence of mineral wealth retarded, to a great extent, the development of the country; but the chief obstacle was the lack of good transport, which prevented such industries as did exist from securing a wide market and a ready outlet for their wares.

To facilitate the movement of troops, after the Rebellion of 1715, some 250 miles of road had been constructed at the expense of the Government; but General Wade, who carried out this work, had only considered the military aspect of the undertaking, and many of his roads were quite unsuited to the requirements of trade operating under peacetime conditions.

In 1803, the Government again took a hand in the betterment of the means of communication. Thomas Telford was appointed to survey for new roads and for the improvement of the existing highways. In the course of the next 17 years he constructed about 920 miles of road, and built some 1,200 bridges.

Following these improvements came the introduction of

numerous stage-coaches, which radiated from Inverness in several directions. By this means the far north was linked with the Highland capital, whence other coaches connected with Aberdeen, and with the industrial districts of the Lowlands.

A partial trade revival resulted. Goods which had previously been borne in coasting vessels could now, in many cases, be sent by road. This meant a considerable saving of time, for the steamship was as yet in its extreme infancy, and bad weather, or contrary winds, often delayed sailing vessels. However, in the Highlands, as in most other parts of the country, it was the railway that most effectually solved the transport problem; but it was many years before the iron road penetrated into these remote districts.

As soon as the steam engine had been proved a success, a number of railways were laid down in the industrial areas of the Lowlands, where trade was good, and the nature of the ground permitted of fairly low constructional costs. There is, however, an old saying that 'The Forth bridles the wild Highlandman'. And just as this had been applied, with some measure of truth, to the raiding clansmen of old, so was it now applicable to the check that the railway received in its advance towards the north. Beyond the River Forth, the well-populated and relatively flat country of the Lowlands gives place to the sterner and wilder Highlands, where large districts are very sparsely inhabited, and where railway construction is a matter of considerable expense.

Along the east coast, however, there is a strip of much easier country, and it was not long before railways were projected in this district, having as their ultimate objective Aberdeen, the largest town on the east coast between Dundee and Inverness, and the trade centre for a wide district. The railway was opened to Perth, from Edinburgh and Glasgow, in 1848, and reached Aberdeen in 1850. For some years the route was made up of the lines of several companies; but eventually all were amalgamated with the Caledonian Railway.

PARLIAMENTARY BATTLE

In March 1845 the Great North of Scotland Railway Company was floated to build a railway from Aberdeen to Inverness. The proposed route went inland from Aberdeen to Elgin, whence it followed the coast, through Forres and Nairn. Branches were to serve Banff, Garmouth, Burghead, and other small fishing townships in Banffshire and Morayshire. This railway, together with the proposed line from Perth to Aberdeen, via Forfar, would have provided a through route, albeit circuitous, between Inverness and the south.

At once two rival schemes were in the field. The first, supported by the inhabitants of the fishing towns which the Great North was to serve by means of branches, was for a railway from Aberdeen to Elgin, passing through Ellon and Turriff to Banff, and following the seaboard from that point. A separate company, the Inverness & Elgin Junction, was to extend the line from Elgin to Inverness, following the same route as that already proposed for the Great North of Scotland Railway. At Inverness a short branch was to serve the harbour.

Neither of these schemes were regarded with any great favour in Inverness. Although both promised reasonably direct access to Aberdeen, the metropolis of the north-east coast, the outlet to the south was deemed unduly circuitous. Small wonder, therefore, that a desire to improve on these projects began to grow. On April 9th, 1845, a prospectus was issued for a direct line across the mountains to Perth. The moving spirit was a civil engineer named Joseph Mitchell, who had worked for several years as Telford's assistant on road construction in the Highlands. Backed by influential Highlanders, he put forward a scheme which, regarded in the light of those early days, was bold in the extreme.

The proposed railway joined the line of the Inverness & Elgin Junction at Nairn, 15 miles east of Inverness, and turning sharply inland, followed the old coach road closely past Ardclach and Glenferness, crossing the Monadhliath

Mountains at an altitude of 1,320 ft above sea level. The line
then ran beside the River Dulnan to Carr Bridge, whence it
turned south to Aviemore. The left bank of the Spey was followed as far as Kingussie, where the river was crossed; and
from Etteridge the railway climbed, to cross the Grampian
Mountains by the Druimuachdar Pass, almost 1,500 ft above
sea level. Beyond the watershed, there was a steep descent beside
the Garry to Blair Atholl, and the Pass of Killiecrankie. The
Tay was crossed near Dunkeld, and the line trended slightly
to the west through the villages of Waterloo and Auchter-
gaven. At Marthall, near Perth, it was proposed to join the
line from Perth to Forfar (the Scottish Midland Junction
Railway) for which a bill already had been deposited. In
addition to the main line, there was to be a spur at Nairn to
enable trains to run direct from Elgin to the south without
reversing. Immediately this scheme was launched, the Inverness & Elgin Junction severed its connexion with the Aberdeen,
Banff & Elgin, and threw in its lot with the new undertaking.

When it is remembered that engineers were then still
imbued with the idea that railways which were to be worked
by pure adhesion must be easily graded, and that huge sums
were frequently expended to attain this ideal, the boldness of
Mitchell's scheme will be readily appreciated. Another fact
that must not be lost sight of, is that between Nairn and Perth,
a distance of almost 120 miles, there were no big towns.
Much of this country was wild, desolate and sparsely inhabited.

All three companies introduced bills into Parliament. At this
stage internal dissensions and grave financial difficulties brought
about the complete collapse of the Aberdeen, Banff & Elgin,
leaving a straight fight between the other two. The advantages
of the direct route, as regards distance, were obvious; but the
long and steep gradients proposed proved an insurmountable
barrier. In the course of the evidence, Mr William Austen, one
of the opposing Parliamentary counsel, is reported to have said:

Ascending such a summit as 1,480 ft is very unprecedented,
and Mr Mitchell is the greatest mountain climber I have

Map of the proposed Inverness & Perth Railway, 1845

ever heard of. He beats Napoleon outright, and quite
eclipses Hannibal. I read a book the other day, of several
hundred pages, describing how Hannibal crossed the Alps.
But after this line will have passed, I have no doubt that
quartos will be written about Mr Mitchell.

The result was that the bill was rejected. Mitchell was a fine
engineer, and a bold thinker; but he was before his time. He
lived to build his railway over the mountains, on a slightly
altered route, it is true, but he had to wait many years before
realizing his dream.

EXPENSIVE VICTORY

The first in the field, the Great North of Scotland Railway, was
successful, and obtained its Act on June 26th, 1846. It is
estimated that the victory cost £80,000; and the Company was
at once in financial straits, which were accentuated by the
crash that followed the 'Railway Mania', then at its height. It
was not until an extension Act had been obtained that work
could be started, on November 25th, 1852.

The railway was opened from Kittybrewster (1½ miles from
Aberdeen) to Huntly, a distance of 39 miles, on September
19th, 1854. Four years previously, the railway had been
completed from Perth to Aberdeen. A through journey was
then made possible between England and the south of Scotland, and Huntly. From this latter point, coaches, running in
connexion with the trains, continued the journey to Inverness.

Here for some time the railway stopped short, want of funds
preventing it from going farther. Subsequently, another Act
was obtained to extend it to Keith, 53 miles from Aberdeen,
and 55 from Inverness. The extension was opened on October
11th, 1856. One year earlier, on September 24th, 1855, the
line had been extended from Kittybrewster to a terminus at
Waterloo Quay, Aberdeen, where a passenger station was
opened on April 1st, 1856. This brought the Great North to

within half a mile of the Guild Street terminus of the line from Perth, an omnibus conveying passengers between the two stations.

Despite frequent overtures to cooperate in the building of a joint station, the Great North remained at Waterloo for 11 years, to the great inconvenience of passengers. Finally, on November 4th, 1867, a short branch was opened from Kitty-brewster to the present joint station. It is only fair to add that this reluctance to participate was caused by the financial difficulties under which the Great North for so long laboured.

It remains to be recorded that in 1847 an Act was obtained for the amalgamation of the Great North and the Aberdeen Railway which formed the connexion to the south. Owing to financial troubles, this was repealed in 1850; and the Aberdeen Railway was later absorbed by the Caledonian. Had this amalgamation Act stood, it is probable that the Highland Railway would never have been built under independent ownership, as the Caledonian would have had a monopoly of the country north of Perth and Aberdeen.

The Great North had won the day in the fight for a railway to the Highlands, but at so great a cost that it was unable to carry out its contract in full. For some years no attempt was made to extend the system west of Keith. Between that town and Elgin lies a stretch of difficult country, and the Company was unable to raise the necessary capital for constructing the railway. Connexions by coach were provided to Inverness, but this was a slow journey, which caused dissatisfaction to all. The Inverness party soon took steps to improve communications in their district; steps that ultimately resulted in the formation of the Highland Railway.

CHAPTER TWO

THE GENESIS OF THE HIGHLAND

THE MISSING LINK TO ABERDEEN

WHEN it became evident that the Great North by its own efforts could not reach Inverness, steps were taken to provide the missing link in the railway to Aberdeen. The Earls of Grant and Seafield took a prominent part in the promotion of the scheme, and on July 24th, 1854, powers were obtained for a railway between Inverness and Nairn, a distance of 15 miles, with a short branch, about half a mile long, to Inverness Harbour. The only real opposition came from Mr Welsh, of Milburn House, close to the terminus of the proposed line. This gentleman claimed that the railway would injure his policies; but his objections were overridden and the construction of the line proceeded.

The first sod was cut by the Countess of Seafield on September 21st, 1854, in the midst of great rejoicings, the day being observed as a general holiday in Inverness. Towards midday a great crowd of people had collected at the Exchange, whence a procession of magistrates, tradesmen and directors of the Company was to proceed to the place where the first sod was to be cut. The scene of the ceremony was a field to the east of Milburn House. Wooden barricades had been erected, but such was the size of the crowd that these proved insufficient, and there was some confusion when many of the spectators broke through and filled up the seats reserved for the distinguished guests.

At length the Countess of Seafield arrived, in company with the young Lord Reidhaven, the Hon Lewis Grant and Dr Edward Macdonald. They were received by Cluny Macpherson, of Cluny, the chairman of the directors. After Dr Macdonald had offered up a prayer, and Cluny had addressed the assembly, the Countess came forward to perform the ceremony of cutting the sod. The special wheelbarrow used for the purpose was made of mahogany, with a bright brass band round the wheel. When the Countess had performed her task, Cluny took the barrow, trundled it to the field, and tipped out the contents, afterwards returning with the empty barrow.

The contractors, Brassey & Falshaw, pushed forward the works with all possible speed, and it was hoped to have the line ready for opening by August 1st, 1855; but many obstacles intervened. All the plant had to be brought by sea, and vexatious delays were frequent by reason of the uncertainty of this means of conveyance. Great trouble was experienced in obtaining delivery of the turntables and signals, and when these did arrive it was found that only part had been sent. There were, however, enough for the formal opening ceremony to take place on November 5th, 1855, official sanction having been obtained on the second.

In honour of the opening, business in the town was almost suspended. The special train was to start at noon, but long before that time a great crowd had collected at the station, an unpretentious building, but described at that time as being neat and designed with the ultimate intention of through communication. The platform was 60 yards long, and it is not surprising that the accommodation was taxed to the utmost. The train consisted of 30 vehicles of various kinds, for the most part ordinary trucks fitted with seats.

Everything being in readiness, the signal to start was given, after the Provost and the magistrates and the directors had taken their seats, and, amidst deafening cheers, the first train left the Highland capital. For the first mile or so the train went very slowly, as vast crowds assembled at the sides of the line. According to one contemporary account:

The people were ranged like a dense hedge on either side, and the welcome they gave the train was most encouraging.

The bridges and heights flanking the seashore were studded with ladies who waved their handkerchiefs. The steep bank, on the summit of which stands the ruin of the Hut of Health, presented a very curious appearance, on account of the crowds of people collected upon it. The number of people could not have been less than two or three thousand, and as they swarmed to see the spectacle, they appeared to hang in black clusters from the banks.

Having passed these crowds, the train gathered speed and travelled at about 30 miles per hour, to the intense excitement and indeed, in some cases, no little fear of the passengers, many of whom had never travelled at this rate before. The train reached Nairn amidst scenes of general rejoicing, and the visitors marched through the town in procession. The return journey began at 3 PM, and Inverness was reached about an hour later, when an immense crowd welcomed the travellers. Public traffic began the next day.

There were four intermediate stations: Culloden, Dalcross, Fort George, and Cawdor. The station at Cawdor served Cawdor Castle; it was renamed Kildrummie in 1857, and disappeared from the public timetables about a year later. Coaches continued to run in connexion with the trains between Nairn and Huntly and later to Keith, when the Great North reached that town. Three train and coach connexions were given in each direction between Inverness and Aberdeen. Between Inverness and Nairn there were three trains each way on weekdays, but this number was soon raised to five. The majority took 45 m. for the journey, calling at all stations; but one, the mail, called only at Fort George, and took 35 m.

Having reached Nairn, no time was lost in pushing on to the east. It was at first proposed to continue as far as Elgin, and wait for the Great North to complete the railway from Keith. As already said, the intervening country is hilly, necessitating some fair-sized earth works, and a costly bridge over the Spey. In consequence, the Great North objected to being left to carry out this section single-handed, and offered the promoters of the Nairn & Elgin £40,000 towards the expense of continuing their line to Keith. This offer was accepted.

The railway, under the title of the Inverness & Aberdeen Junction, was authorized between Nairn and Keith on July 21st, 1856, and was to take over the working of the Inverness & Nairn. Amalgamation between the two took place on May 17th, 1861.

The first section, 8 miles long, was opened from Nairn to Dalvey on December 22nd, 1857. Dalvey station stood on the west bank of the Findhorn, near Forres. It was a temporary terminus, and was only in use pending the completion of the bridge over the river. When this was finished, the station was closed on March 25th, 1858, on which date the line was opened to Elgin. On August 18th following, Keith was reached, and a through journey between Inverness and Aberdeen was for the first time possible.

The most noteworthy engineering feat on the line was the bridge over the Spey at Orton. For some time after the railway was opened to Keith, it was in an unfinished state, a temporary scaffolding carrying the rails, and the Board of Trade would not sanction its use for passenger trains. Accordingly, on the arrival of the train, the passengers got out and walked over the adjacent road bridge. The engine was detached, and the coaches hauled over by ropes. The passengers having re-entrained, a fresh locomotive was attached and the train continued its journey. The bridge was rebuilt in 1906.

THE MORAYSHIRE RAILWAY

Closely associated with the Inverness & Aberdeen Junction Railway was a local undertaking, the Morayshire Railway, which, after a somewhat chequered history, passed into the hands of the Great North of Scotland Railway. In 1841 a survey was made for a railway between Elgin and the fishing port of Lossiemouth, a distance of 6 miles. But the scheme failed for lack of support. Some years later it was revived under the title of the Morayshire Railway, and a bill was submitted to Parliament in 1846.

At the same time, the Great North of Scotland Railway was seeking powers for the line from Aberdeen to Inverness. It was proposed to connect the two railways at Elgin and to build an extension of the Morayshire from Orton, 10 miles to the east, to Rothes and Craigellachie, in Strathspey, leaving the main line of the Great North to provide the connecting link. Powers for the complete undertaking were obtained on July 16th, 1846, a few weeks after the Great North of Scotland Act had been passed.

When, owing to the financial crash, the Great North decided to limit its undertaking to a line from Aberdeen to Keith, the directors of the Morayshire applied to the Railway Commissioners for permission to abandon their extension to Craigellachie, and a warrant authorizing this action was granted on July 10th, 1851. The first sod of the Elgin–Lossiemouth section was cut in the following November, and the railway was opened on August 10th, 1852.

By 1856, proposals were afoot for the completion of the Craigellachie extension under the sole ownership of the Morayshire Company; but with the advent of the Inverness & Aberdeen Junction Railway it was decided to revert to the original scheme of 1846, and make use of that Company's track between Elgin and Orton. On July 14th, 1856, the Company was once more authorized to construct the extension. The line was opened from Orton to Rothes, $3\frac{1}{2}$ miles, on August 23rd, 1858, and to Craigellachie* on December 23rd following.

For a few weeks Morayshire trains worked separately between Elgin and Orton; but soon it became the practice to attach the coaches to Inverness & Aberdeen Junction trains. In all probability, lightness of traffic was a deciding factor in this alteration; but it was subsequently alleged to have been necessary because of the serious delays to main-line trains, caused by the constant failure of the Morayshire engines.

The agreement for the common use of the line between Elgin

* Actually Dandaleith, on the west bank of the Spey.

and Orton involved the two companies in a serious dispute destined to have far-reaching results. The Morayshire claimed the right to carry passengers and goods from places on its own system to stations on the Inverness & Aberdeen Junction Railway, served by the trains of both companies, paying only a proportion of the fare for use of track and haulage. The latter Company retorted that such traffic should pass completely into its hands at Elgin or Orton, and that the proportional rates applied only to traffic from Lossiemouth to Rothes and Craigellachie, or *vice versa*. Matters came to a head when the Inverness & Aberdeen Junction Railway attempted to seize the traffic at the junctions, and the Morayshire Railway decided to seek powers for an independent line.

The Act authorizing the railway from Elgin to Rothes, through the Glen of Rothes, was passed on July 3rd, 1860. The junction at Elgin faced away from Lossiemouth, necessitating a reversal for through trains. The line was opened on January 1st, 1862. For some time connexions were given between Rothes and Orton, but except for passengers proceeding eastwards towards Keith this section became redundant.

On May 17th, 1861, the Morayshire Railway was empowered to extend its line over the Spey at Craigellachie and effect a junction with the Strathspey Railway, which was authorized on the same date from Dufftown to Grantown-on-Spey. At Dufftown this latter line joined the Keith & Dufftown, which was in effect an extension of the Great North of Scotland Railway. Now, that Company had contributed to the building of all three of the local lines, and ultimately concluded working agreements with them on July 30th, 1866, thus providing for itself a through route to Elgin. In the case of the Morayshire, the Great North was to work the line at 45 per cent, and this arrangement continued until complete amalgamation in 1881.

On the day following the working agreement (July 31st, 1866), the Great North, without notice, closed the section between Orton and Rothes, as being no longer required. This action was the subject of some discussion between the two companies, but the dispute was finally settled to the satisfaction of both. The abandoned section remained for many years just as it had been left, and became much overgrown. The permanent way was not removed until 1907. The course of the line remained plainly visible, particularly at Orton, where the junction with the line to Keith was very clearly defined.

Mention must be made of the Findhorn Railway, another small line now consigned to the limbo of forgotten ventures. It served the village of Findhorn, on the eastern shores of the bay of the same name, about 5 miles north-east of Forres.

On April 19th, 1859, an Act was obtained for the construction of a railway, 3 miles long, from the village to a junction with the Inverness & Aberdeen Junction Railway at Kinloss. There were no constructional difficulties, as the surrounding country was level and sandy. The railway was opened on April 18th, 1860, and was worked as an independent concern for two years. At the end of this period the Company found itself in financial difficulties, and on March 1st, 1862, the line was taken over by the Inverness & Aberdeen Junction Railway, and worked as a branch of that system. Traffic still proved insufficient to pay operating expenses, and regular services were withdrawn on January 1st, 1869.

For the time being, occasional goods trains were run, but the line was completely closed about 1880, and the Company was wound up. The permanent way was removed, but the course of the line remained clearly traceable, particularly at the northern end, where the railway ran in a shallow cutting between the main street of the village and the shore. The terminus was at the quayside, and to facilitate the loading of ships a siding, approached by a wagon turntable, was laid on the pier. The platform and station buildings were demolished, the site being eventually occupied by some sheds. One of the chief causes of the failure of the railway was the difficult approach to the harbour at Findhorn. At its mouth the river forms a huge landlocked bay, but the sea has thrown up a sand-bar, making the entrance difficult and restricting the size of ships. The sand subsequently accumulated to such an extent that the harbour was practically closed.

INCONVENIENCE AT ABERDEEN

At long last Inverness had secured a railway route to the south, but the undertaking left many things to be desired. By reason of the £40,000 subscribed, directors of the Great North of Scotland Railway attended the board meetings of the other Company. Despite the fact that they had failed in their original undertaking, and had only been able to render partial assistance in the building of more than half the line between Aberdeen and Inverness, they adopted a high-handed attitude which resulted in constant friction between the two companies. Finally, in 1860, the Inverness & Aberdeen Junction Railway bought out the Great North, and was left to manage its own affairs.

Far worse than those boardroom quarrels was the inconvenience at Aberdeen, caused by the two stations at Waterloo and Guild Street being over half a mile apart. On arrival at Guild Street of the mail train from the south, the mails were at once transferred to a waiting van and taken to Waterloo. Passengers and luggage followed by omnibus. There was a margin of about three-quarters of an hour between the arrival of the train from Perth and the departure for Inverness, and if the train from the south was punctual, a good connexion could be made. Frequently, however, the train from Perth arrived late. In this case, the mails were at once rushed over to Waterloo, and as soon as they were loaded, the Great North started the train.

If the passengers could reach Waterloo station as soon as the mails, for which the Great North was bound to wait, and could get into the train before they were loaded, they were certain of their connexion. But the train was often started before the passengers could arrive, or before they could all transfer from the omnibus to the train, and travellers were stranded.

There is a picturesque story to the effect that on one occasion, when the train from the south was late, the omnibus was seen tearing along the quay in the wake of the mail van. As soon as this latter arrived, although it wanted still a few minutes to starting time, the officials shut and bolted the doors of the station against the omnibus, rather than delay their train, which was duly started, despite the knockings and clamourings of the furious passengers without. It is said that amongst these were certain influential Highlanders, and that, enraged by such high-handed treatment, they held an indignation meeting, and there and then decided to promote another direct line to the south, and obviate changing and discourtesy.

Whether or no the above story is true is a moot point. There is no question, however, that the connexion was frequently missed through passengers arriving at Waterloo after starting time. The Inverness party was never satisfied with the circuitous route via Aberdeen, and it needed but little to revive the project for a direct line over the mountains to Perth. Joseph Mitchell was again called upon to survey a route, and, after much negotiation with the landowners, a bill was submitted to Parliament in November 1860.

CHAPTER THREE

ACROSS THE GRAMPIANS

AGITATION FOR A DIRECT ROUTE

As EARLY as 1845, the Scottish Midland Junction Railway promoted a branch through Strathtay to Dunkeld, but by mutual consent the proposal made way for the ill-fated direct line from Inverness to Perth. Although the Scottish Midland Junction reinstated its bill, which was duly passed, construction was never begun, and the scheme lapsed. Finally, on July 10th, 1854, an independent company, the Perth & Dunkeld, obtained an Act for a line, 8¼ miles long, leaving the Scottish Midland Junction at Stanley, 7¼ miles from Perth, and terminating at Birnam, on the opposite side of the Tay from Dunkeld. The railway was opened on April 7th, 1856, and was worked first by the Scottish Midland Junction, and subsequently by the Scottish North Eastern Railway.*

Four years later, with the renewal of the agitation for a shortened route from Inverness to the south, the importance of this purely local undertaking increased. The proposed new railway through the Central Highlands left the Inverness & Aberdeen Junction Railway at Forres, 24 miles east of Inverness, and turning sharply to the south, rose steeply for several miles to cross the hills separating the valley of the Findhorn from Strathspey. Beyond the summit at Dava, 1,052 ft above sea level, the approximate course of the route surveyed by Mitchell in 1845 was joined, and the line proceeded by way of Grantown and the west bank of the Spey to Kingussie. There followed a long, steep climb up the northern slopes of the

---

*The Scottish North Eastern Railway was formed on July 29th, 1856, by an amalgamation between the Scottish Midland Junction and Aberdeen Railways.

Grampians to the head of the Druimuachdar Pass, and a corresponding descent to Blair Atholl and the Pass of Killie-crankie. Crossing the Tay near Dalguise, the line reached Dunkeld, where it made an end-on junction with the Perth & Dunkeld Railway.

Although the route was characterized by its severe gradients, and the summit level of 1,484 ft at Druimuachdar exceeded any previously sanctioned in the British Isles, such had been the advance in locomotive design since 1845 that the arguments which had secured the rejection of Mitchell's original plans now proved unavailing. Despite determined opposition, the Act was passed on July 22nd, 1861.* By the terms of the Act, the Company, under the title of the Inverness & Perth Junction Railway, was to take over the Perth & Dunkeld Railway. The two systems were amalgamated on February 28th, 1864.

The first sod was cut on October 17th, 1861, and so expeditiously was the work carried out that the 13 miles from Dunkeld to Pitlochry were opened on June 1st, 1863. The 36 miles from Forres to Aviemore followed on August 3rd, and the final length over the Grampians, from Aviemore to Pitlochry, was completed on September 9th.

The chief engineering works on the line were the seven-span masonry viaduct over the Divie, near Dunphail, 477 ft long and 105 ft high; the girder bridge across the Tay, near Dalguise, 515 ft long and 67 ft high; and the ten-span masonry viaduct, 54 ft high, over a deep ravine in the Pass of Killiecrankie. Smaller masonry bridges were required to carry the railway over the Bran, north of Dunkeld, and the Garry, at Struan. The latter was remarkable in that its main span crossed not

* Thus Druimuachdar became the highest summit on a standard gauge railway in the country, the North Eastern Railway's mineral line at Parkhead (Blanchland), opened in 1834, having reached 1,474 ft above sea level. When the Leadhills Light Railway (worked by the Caledonian) was opened in 1902, both these heights were eclipsed by a new record, 1,498 ft. Closure of the Light Railway in 1939 restored the *status quo ante*. Blanchland has since closed, leaving Druimuachdar in first place.

only the river, but also the stone bridge carrying the Rannoch Road over the Garry at the same point. At Blair Atholl the Tilt was crossed by a single-span lattice-girder bridge.

Only two short tunnels were found necessary – one in the Pass of Killiecrankie (128 yds long), and the other north of Dunkeld (350 yds long). South of Dunkeld there was a third tunnel (310 yds long), but this had, of course, been constructed by the Perth & Dunkeld Railway. (These, incidentally, were the only three tunnels on the Highland Railway.)

Although the work of building the main line was completed as soon as possible, some time elapsed before all the stations were ready to be opened, a few of the smaller ones being left until communication between Forres and Perth had been established. Thus accommodation was not provided at Dava until 1864, and Killiecrankie and Dalnaspidal until 1865.

On the other hand, two stations subsequently closed figured in the timetables. One was at Rohallion, between Murthly and Dunkeld, serving the castle of the same name. Opened by the Perth & Dunkeld Railway, the train service consisted, for some time, of one train in each direction, on Fridays only. Later on, this was increased to a daily train in each direction. It would appear, however, that the station was in the nature of a conditional halting-place, as the early timetables have the following note appended: 'Stops by request at Rohallion, Dunkeld fares charged'. The sparseness of the traffic brought about the closing of the platform in 1864. Almost all traces of the station have disappeared, and it is now difficult to identify the site.

The second station subsequently closed was at Rafford, between Dunphail and Forres, at a point where a side road from the village of Rafford crossed the railway. A complete station was established here, and not a conditional stopping-place as at Rohallion. However, traffic did not come up to expectations, and it was closed in 1865. Until 1871 the station subsequently known as Kincraig was named Boat of Insh, taking its name from the nearby 'boat', or ferry, over the River Insh.

A new station was required at Forres. A double junction was
provided with the line from Inverness to Keith, so that trains
could be run in each direction without reversing. To give each
train platform accommodation, a new station, triangular in
form, was built to the south of the existing one. A new line
was provided for the trains from east to west, leaving the
original route as an auxiliary loop for goods trains and light
engines. The old station building became the stationmaster's
residence.

The junctions at Forres

The 1861 Act also authorized a branch, 9 miles long, from
Ballinluig to Aberfeldy, along the valley of the Tay. Powers for
a similar line had been obtained in 1846 by a small independent
company, the Strathtay & Breadalbane, but the rejection of
the bill for the direct line from Inverness to Perth had caused
the scheme to fall into abeyance. Work on this section was
considerably delayed, and it was not until July 3rd, 1865, that
it was ready to be opened. It was an expensive line to construct.
There were 41 bridges, including two over the river, and
800,000 cubic yds of cutting and filling were required.

THE IMPORTANCE OF PERTH

The advantages of the direct line were many. It eliminated the changing and discourtesy at Aberdeen, and gave a route virtually under one ownership between Inverness and Perth. The greatest benefit lay, however, in the shortening of the journey. Previously the distance by rail from Perth to Inverness had been 198 miles; it now became 144. This represented a saving of about 2¾ hours in travelling time, and a corresponding reduction in fares.

As early as 1848 Perth had become a railway centre of considerable importance; and by the Scottish Central Railway's Act of that year the railways converging on the town were authorized to contribute towards the provision of a general station on that Company's line. In 1861 the Inverness & Perth Junction Railway was granted running powers over the Scottish North Eastern Railway, between Stanley Junction and Perth, and the right of user of the general station. Four years later the interests of the various companies were vested in a joint committee, which took over the entire management of the station. As the result of the amalgamations in 1865 and 1866 between the Caledonian, the Scottish Central and the Scottish North Eastern Railways, the number of partners in the undertaking was reduced to three: the Caledonian, the North British and the Highland, with the predominant interest in the hands of the Caledonian. The Station Hotel was the subject of a separate Act in 1865.

Although the Inverness & Perth Junction Railway was assured of the right to use the station, both by the Act of 1861 and the subsequent setting up of the joint committee, some difficulty was experienced with the Scottish North Eastern Railway over the question of tolls for the use of the line between Stanley and Perth. For some time after the line was opened, the Inverness & Perth Junction paid toll on each passenger, and as the traffic grew, this amount reached large proportions. The owning company was repeatedly approached with a view to a settlement whereby this toll could either be considerably reduced, or a fixed sum paid each year, but for some time the parties were unable to reach a basis of agreement.

At the half-yearly shareholders' meeting in 1866, it was reported that a survey had been made for an independent route between Stanley and Perth, which would not only obviate the necessity of paying anything, but which was slightly shorter than the existing line. This threat evidently brought the Scottish North Eastern into a more reasonable frame of mind, for, at the meeting in the following year, it was announced that after the tolls had reached the high total of £10,000 in the previous year, the two companies had come to an agreement whereby the Inverness & Perth Junction Railway was to pay the sum of £5,000 per annum in perpetuity, irrespective of the number of passengers that passed over the line. The Scottish North Eastern Railway also undertook not to divert an undue amount of traffic over the older route, via Aberdeen.

Some time prior to the opening of the direct line to Perth, a further addition was made to the Inverness & Aberdeen Junction Railway in the shape of a branch from Alves to the fishing port of Burghead, a distance of 5½ miles. It will be remembered that the original scheme of the Great North of Scotland Railway had included a branch to Burghead, but it was not until 17 years later that the village obtained railway facilities. Powers were obtained on May 17th, 1861, to construct the branch, which was opened on December 22nd, 1862, to a station on Burghead Pier. In 1864 a station was opened at Wards between Alves and Burghead, at which trains called by request. In the following year the name was changed to Coltfield Platform.

THE HIGHLAND RAILWAY IS BORN

Following the opening of the direct line to Perth came a period of amalgamation and consolidation. Amalgamation had already taken place, on May 17th, 1861, between the Inverness & Nairn and the Inverness & Aberdeen Junction Railways, and on February 28th, 1864, between the Inverness & Perth Junction and Perth & Dunkeld Railways. One year later, on February 1st, 1865, the Inverness & Aberdeen Junction and the Inverness & Perth Junction Railways were amalgamated. On June 29th following, the combined undertaking was authorized to be known as the Highland Railway, with headquarters at Inverness. At the time of its inception the Company owned, or worked, 242 route miles, made up as follows:

Inverness to Keith	...	...	...	55 miles
Forres to Stanley	...	...	...	111¾ ,,
*Inverness to Bonar Bridge	...	...	57½ ,,
Ballinluig to Aberfeldy	...	...	...	8¾ ,,
Alves to Burghead	...	...	...	5½ ,,
†Kinloss to Findhorn	...	...	...	3½ ,,
Total	...	...	...	242 miles

*See Chapter 4.
† Worked since 1862 by the Inverness & Aberdeen Junction Railway.

The 7¼ miles of Scottish North Eastern track between Stanley Junction and Perth should be added to obtain the total of 249¼ miles over which the Company's trains actually worked.

CHAPTER FOUR

THE ADVANCE TO THE NORTH

THE GEOGRAPHICAL OBSTACLE

IN CERTAIN respects, the geographical position of Inverness is similar to that of Edinburgh. Immediately to the north of the latter is the Firth of Forth, about 5 miles wide directly opposite the city, but narrowing considerably towards the west. Beyond comes the somewhat isolated peninsula county of Fife, bounded on the north by the Firth of Tay, about 2 miles wide at Dundee.

To the north of the Highland capital is the Beauly Firth, about 1½ miles wide in most places, but narrowing to about half a mile, at Kessock Ferry, close to the city. The analogy to Fife is supplied by the peninsula of the Black Isle, while the Cromarty Firth corresponds to the Firth of Tay. Here, however, the similarity ends. In the south there are no more deep indentations of the coast as far as Aberdeen, but north of the Cromarty Firth is a third big opening, the Dornoch Firth, running deeper into the land than the other two. A few miles north of the Dornoch Firth is Loch Fleet, but this is a much smaller opening and does not constitute a particularly serious obstacle.

For many years a railway journey from Edinburgh to Dundee was a very roundabout business, and it was not until 1890 that both the Firths of Forth and Tay were bridged, and a direct line of communication established. Fortunately, the volume of traffic rendered such costly structures desirable. In the case of Inverness, however, not only did the original railways have to run round the arms of the sea, but subsequently the traffic did not increase to an extent to warrant the provision of any deviations to shorten the route. As the crow flies, the distance from Inverness to Wick is about 80 miles; by the railway it is 161 miles. Moreover, the only places of any size are situated on the east coast, so that any railway between Inverness and the far north would have, of necessity, to follow the coast, with its windings, in order to serve these trade centres.

THE INVERNESS & ROSS-SHIRE RAILWAY

Soon after the Inverness & Nairn Railway was opened, the possibility of an extension to the north was mooted. Some difficulty was experienced in the choice of a route, and several suggestions were put forward. The supporters of one scheme proposed to establish a steamer service between Nairn and the north side of the Cromarty Firth, whence one railway was to be built to Tain, and another to Invergordon, and possibly to Dingwall. It was not at that time considered practicable to build a railway from Inverness to Dingwall, via Beauly, because of the great expense of bridging the River Ness and the Caledonian Canal, and the Rivers Beauly and Conon. This scheme never came to fruition; and finally, an all-railway route between Inverness and the north was proposed.

The moving spirit of the undertaking was Sir Alexander Matheson, of Ardross, who worked unceasingly to obtain the line. His efforts resulted in the passing of the Inverness & Ross-shire Railway's Act, on July 3rd, 1860, for a railway from Inverness to Invergordon, a distance of 31 miles.

The ceremony of cutting the first sod was performed on September 19th, 1860, by Lady Matheson, the day being observed as a general holiday in Inverness. At 3 PM the procession, headed by the Militia, started for the field, which was situated opposite the 'White House', on the outskirts of the town, where Meakin, the contractor for the Inverness–Dingwall section, was awaiting its arrival. After the ceremony, the party returned to the town, and in the evening the directors of the new line were entertained to dinner.

The construction of the railway was pushed forward with all possible speed. In December 1861, Miss Mitchell, daughter of the engineer, laid the keystone of the Ness Viaduct, and the swing-bridge over the Caledonian Canal, at Clachnaharry, was completed shortly afterwards. The last of the big works to be finished was the masonry viaduct over the River Conon, although the foundation stone had been laid by Miss MacKenzie, of Seaforth, as early as November, 1860. The Beauly River was crossed by a timber bridge (renewed as a steel structure in 1909). In March 1861 the contract for the 13 miles from Dingwall to Invergordon was let to MacDonald & Grieve, with the stipulation that the work should be completed as soon as that between Inverness and Dingwall, so that the whole railway could be opened at the same time. The date fixed for the opening was April 1st, 1862, but unforeseen delays occurred.

The opening of the section between Inverness and Dingwall took place on June 11th, 1862. On the previous day the line had been inspected by Colonel Yolland, of the Board of Trade, who expressed entire satisfaction with all the works. The directors thereupon decided to open the line on the following day, Andrew Dougall, the secretary, announcing the fact by wire from Dingwall, and ordering a special train to leave that evening with all the officials, who were to be dropped at their respective stations in readiness for the opening on the morrow.

The existing terminus at Inverness was not adapted for conversion to a through station, as it faced south, with a frontage in Academy Street, whereas the new line approached the city from the west. It was therefore decided to enlarge the station by the provision of extra terminal platforms on the west side to accommodate the Ross-shire trains. The two railways diverged immediately beyond the station, passing on either side of the locomotive shops. The third side of the triangle, providing physical connexion from east to west, was formed by part of the harbour branch. This line subsequently became known as the Rose Street curve.

Although further additions were made to the station from

time to time, until there were four platforms in the southern section, and three in the northern, the layout remained practically unaltered. The somewhat unusual arrangement of lines proved convenient as, apart from a few through coaches, Inverness was the terminus of all trains arriving. To facilitate the interchange of passengers, it became the practice to send trains from the south via the Rose Street curve, whence they were reversed into the northern part of the station. A similar procedure was adopted with arrivals from the north, but trains from the Keith line usually ran direct to a platform in the southern section.

The completion of the line from Dingwall to Invergordon was much delayed by the opposition of Mr MacKenzie, of Findon, who claimed that his tenants would be placed in danger if they had to use the proposed level crossing on the Ferry Road. After much discussion, the Company decided on a bridge, and the railway was opened on March 25th, 1863.

Shortly after the opening of the line to Dingwall, the Inverness & Ross-shire Railway was amalgamated with the Inverness & Aberdeen Junction Railway, the Act authorizing the union being dated June 30th, 1862. By the Ross-shire Extension Act, passed on May 11th, 1863, powers were obtained to extend the line to Bonar Bridge, 26½ miles from Invergordon, and 57½ from Inverness. The railway was opened to Meikle Ferry, 2½ miles from Tain, on June 1st, 1864, and to Bonar Bridge on October 1st following.

The temporary terminus at Meikle Ferry provides another instance of stations that have subsequently been closed. It was situated at a point where a tongue of land juts out into the Dornoch Firth, and the narrow strait thus formed is crossed by a ferry. Some 4 miles to the north is Dornoch, the county town of Sutherland, and one of the smallest county towns in the country. The ferry not only gives easier access to Dornoch, but also to places lying farther to the north, as the nearest road bridge over the firth is at Bonar Bridge, some miles to the west.

When the railway reached Meikle Ferry, a coach connected, via the ferry, with towns and villages in Sutherland and

Caithness. But the ferry was some distance from the station and a journey to the north by this route was naturally somewhat slow. When the railway was completed to Bonar Bridge, coach connexions were still given via the ferry, but this lasted for a short time only as they soon began to operate from Bonar Bridge. In consequence, traffic at the ferry station dwindled almost to vanishing point. The station was closed in 1869.

Between Edderton and Bonar Bridge a station known as Mid Fearn was provided to serve Fearn Lodge. It remained open for only eleven months, after which it was withdrawn from the public timetables, although still used as a conditional stopping-place for the lodge and the wives and families of local railwaymen.

Another station worthy of mention is Clachnaharry, situated close to the bridge over the Caledonian Canal. Opened in 1869, it remained in continuous use until it was closed in 1913. There was no station at Clunes until 1864, and in 1869 Parkhill station was renamed Kildary, to avoid confusion with the Aberdeenshire station of the same name, on the Great North of Scotland Railway.

THE SUTHERLAND AND THE
DUKE OF SUTHERLAND'S RAILWAYS

The village of Bonar Bridge is in two portions, one on each side of the Kyle of Sutherland, as the upper reaches of the Dornoch Firth are called. On the north, or Sutherland, side is Bonar Bridge proper, while on the Ross-shire side is Ardgay, and the railway station of Bonar Bridge. The two portions of the village are connected by a long road bridge which carries the main road to the north over the kyle. When an extension of the railway was proposed, it was decided to continue on the south side of the kyle for some 3 miles, crossing thence to the northern shore to follow the banks of the River Shin and the course of the River Fleet down to the coast, at the head of Loch Fleet.

On June 29th, 1865, the Sutherland Railway was authorized from Bonar Bridge to Brora, a distance of 32¾ miles. Having crossed the kyle, the railway climbed through the hills to Lairg, at the south-eastern end of Loch Shin, whence roads radiate in several directions to the west and north coasts. Turning to the east, the line continued past the head of Loch Fleet to Golspie and Brora.

Plan of Inverness station

Despite a contribution of £15,000 by the Highland Railway, the promoters were unable to carry out the whole of their scheme. The works were heavy and expensive, especially the viaduct over the kyle, comprising five masonry arches and a girder span of 230 ft, and the rock cuttings near Lairg. On April 13th, 1868, the 26 miles from Bonar Bridge to Golspie were opened. A service of coaches, running in connexion with the trains, was established between Golspie and Wick and Thurso, and between the Mound (at the head of Loch Fleet) and Dornoch.

For some years there was no station between Bonar Bridge and Invershin, at the northern end of the bridge over the Kyle of Sutherland. The nearest road bridge was at Ardgay, and people living on the Ross-shire side of the kyle had to come into Bonar Bridge to join the train, although the railway passed almost by their doors. A great improvement was effected in 1871, when a platform was opened at Culrain, at the south end of the viaduct. For the time being, trains stopped by request to pick up or set down passengers; but by 1873 it figured in the timetables as an ordinary station. Although only 36 chains apart, Culrain and Invershin served different districts, because of the lack of facilities for crossing the kyle. (Prior to January 1st, 1917, a third-class single ticket between these stations cost one halfpenny, the lowest fare on the Highland Railway.) In contrast to this distance were the 10 miles separating Lairg and Rogart.

The Sutherland Railway had stopped short at Golspie, and the next advance in the extension towards the north was made possible by the generosity of the Duke of Sutherland, the principal land-owner in the county, whose seat was at Dunrobin Castle, 2 miles north of Golspie. Since the creation of the title in 1833, successive Dukes had done much to better conditions in the county and expended considerable sums on various improvement schemes. Large tracts of moorland were reclaimed and turned into fertile farm lands, while in the west and north of the county new roads were made in the neighbourhoods of Durness and Lochinver.

As soon as the railway reached Golspie, the third Duke projected a privately-owned line along the coast for some 17 miles to Helmsdale, on the borders of Caithness. The railway was to come close to Dunrobin Castle, and pass onwards through Brora, the originally-intended terminus of the Sutherland Railway, serving a number of flourishing fishing villages. The Act authorizing the transfer to the new undertaking of the 6 miles of the Sutherland Company's line from Golspie to Brora, and the extension of the railway from Brora to Helmsdale, was passed on June 20th, 1870, but construction had begun before the powers were obtained.

Engineering difficulties at either end of the line delayed the completion of the works, but the section from Dunrobin (2 miles north of Golspie) to a point about three-quarters of a mile short of Helmsdale was finished by the autumn of 1870. The Duke decided that the railway should be opened forthwith, and a temporary station, known as West Helmsdale, was built at Gartymore. An engine and some coaches were purchased for working the line, but since there was as yet no physical connexion with the Sutherland Railway, at Golspie, the stock had to be placed on wagons and hauled along the road by a traction engine.

The opening ceremony was performed on November 1st, 1870, by Princess Christian, and for the next seven months a service of two trains a day in each direction was run. By that time the works were completed, and on June 19th, 1871, the railway was opened throughout, and the Highland Railway took over the working.

The temporary terminus at Dunrobin became a private station serving the castle, at which trains called by request to pick up or set down passengers. In 1902 the buildings were reconstructed to the designs of the estate architect.

ON TO THE FAR NORTH

Caithness, the most northerly county in Scotland, has only two towns of any size: Wick, situated on the east coast, and, some 20 miles away, Thurso, on the north coast. The former is a flourishing port for the herring fishery, while the latter, beside boasting a not inconsiderable connexion with the fishing industry, is the nearest port on the mainland to the Orkneys.

In the early 1860s a railway was proposed between the two towns, and after many delays the line was authorized on July 30th, 1866. The Company, under the title of the Caithness Railway, was to build a line from Wick to Thurso, with a view to an extension (to be authorized at a later date) to join the Sutherland Railway, which had obtained its Act one year previously for a railway from Bonar Bridge to Brora.

The line as authorized was only a local undertaking, isolated from the railway system of the rest of the country. For the most part, the proposed southern extension would have passed through desolate country, boasting but few inhabitants. Despite the efforts of local landlords to raise the money, the necessary funds were not forthcoming, and for many years the whole scheme was in abeyance, the Company being unable to commence even the 21 miles between Wick and Thurso, where the country is relatively fertile.

The distance from Helmsdale to Wick along the east coast is about 35 miles, but the high land round the Ord of Caithness prevents a railway from keeping to the shore and forces it inland. The road, it is true, follows the east coast, but it is carried over the Ord by means of long hills. There is also a precipitous drop into the village of Berriedale, with a corresponding rise on the other side. The proposed extension of the Caithness Railway was intended to run inland from Helmsdale to a point about 8 miles from Thurso, where it was to join the already sanctioned railway from Wick to Thurso.

Meanwhile, thanks to the efforts of the Duke of Sutherland, the railway was being extended from Golspie to Helmsdale, and a new company, the Sutherland & Caithness, was formed to carry the railway on from Helmsdale to the north. The new concern proposed to take over the Caithness Railway, and to follow the same route, both as regards the section already authorized, and the southern extension. The latter joined the Thurso–Wick line at Georgemas, which thus became the most northerly junction in the British Isles. The Act authorizing construction was passed on July 13th, 1871, and the railway was opened on July 28th, 1874.* The Highland Railway subscribed £50,000 and the Duke of Sutherland £60,000.

North of Helmsdale, in sparsely-inhabited Strath Ullie, the stations were placed some distance apart. When the railway was first opened, 9½ miles separated Helmsdale and Kildonan, and 8¼ Kildonan and Kinbrace. In 1877 a platform and siding was opened to serve Borrobol shooting lodge, which lies close

*Hoy Station was not opened until October 1st.

to the railway, about 2 miles north of Kildonan; trains called by request to pick up or set down. In July 1907 a second platform, similar to Borrobol, was opened at Salzcraggie, between Helmsdale and Kildonan, to serve Salzcraggie Lodge. Both were advertised as normal public stopping places, although Salzcraggie was officially a private station, maintained at the expense of the owner of Salzcraggie Lodge.

THE DINGWALL & SKYE RAILWAY

Although no efforts were spared to carry the railway through to the shores of the Pentland Firth, the possibilities of a branch to the west coast, north of the Caledonian Canal, were not overlooked. Because of the mountainous configuration of the country, there are only certain routes along which a crossing from east to west can be made. From very early times, these passes through the hills have been used for roads, and any railways crossing the country must of necessity follow approximately the same route. One of these natural highways runs westwards from Dingwall, the county town of Ross-shire, up Strath Conon and Strath Bran. Thence it passes over the watershed into Strath Carron. The coast is reached at a point opposite the Isle of Skye, on the sheltered waters of the Inner Sound. The distance from sea to sea is a little over 60 miles. The western end of this road forms a convenient port for the Isle of Skye and the Outer Hebrides.

About 1863 a proposal was made for a railway along this route to the west coast. Two years later the idea took definite shape, and powers were granted on July 5th, 1865, for a railway 63 miles long, from the Highland Railway at Dingwall to Kyle of Lochalsh. The route ran due west for about 4 miles to the village of Strathpeffer Spa, whose mineral springs had already become widely known. The high ground lying to the north-west of Strathpeffer was to be avoided by trending somewhat to the south, through the village of Contin, to the banks of the Blackwater River, and the line then passed

through Garve, and along the side of Loch Luichart to Strath
Bran, whence it ran westwards to the coast. The Highland
Railway was to subscribe £50,000 and the Caledonian Railway
£100,000.

Unfortunately, the landowners in the Strathpeffer district
put up the most determined opposition. Foremost among
them was Sir William MacKenzie, of Coul House. The proposed railway passed through his lands for about 4 miles, and
came to within a quarter of a mile of the house. At the Company's meeting in October 1866 it was reported that unexpected difficulties with regard to the purchase of the land had
arisen, and that pending a settlement of these disputes nothing
would be done towards the construction of the line. Matters
remained at this impasse for some 3 years. Finally, on May
29th, 1868, a further Act was obtained which sanctioned
various deviations.

The Strathpeffer difficulty was overcome by diverting the
railway somewhat to the north, so that it passed about 2 miles
from the spa. Not only did this deprive Strathpeffer of a
railway station in a central position, but the new location gave
the railway a 4-mile climb, for the most part at 1 in 50, to the
Raven Rock Summit, whereas the original route would have
been less severely graded. There is a tragic side to the story.
Sir William MacKenzie did not enjoy his victory, as he died
shortly before the line was finished.

The other alteration sanctioned by the Act of 1868 was at the
western end of the railway. Because of the enormous cost of
construction between Strome Ferry and Kyle of Lochalsh, it
was decided to abandon that section. This had the effect of
moving the terminus some 10 miles up the sea-water Loch
Carron. Ships could reach Strome Ferry, but Loch Carron
was not such an ideal harbour as Kyle, being subject to strong
currents and tides. There can be no doubt, however, that for
the time being the Company was justified in taking this step.

The railway was opened throughout in 1870 – for goods on
August 5th and for passengers on August 19th. On the same
day steamers began to run from the new pier at Strome Ferry

to Portree, in the Isle of Skye, and to Stornoway in Lewis. The new railway opened up a quicker route between the islands and the south. Previously, passengers and goods had to go right round by sea to the Clyde, but the journey time was now reduced by many hours. In addition, the north-east of Scotland was for the first time made easily accessible from the Hebrides.

Several years elapsed before all the stations on the Skye line were open. Lochluichart and Achnashellach were added in 1871; Glencarron Platform followed in 1873; but Attadale was not opened until 1880.

To complete the early history of the northern lines, mention must be made of the branch to the Muirtown Basin of the Caledonian Canal, about 1 mile from Inverness. To facilitate traffic between the basin and the town, a branch 58 chains long was constructed from Canal Junction, on the northern main line, to the wharf, and opened on April 9th, 1877. Not until July 4th, 1890, was official sanction obtained. Although the branch was extensively used by goods trains, the proposed passenger service, running in connexion with the steamers on the canal, was never provided.

AMALGAMATION OF THE NORTHERN LINES

Twelve years had sufficed to bring the railway from Inverness up the east coast to the extreme north of the mainland and across the country from sea to sea. When the sparseness of the population and the meagre traffic are considered, this represents no mean achievement. From its inception, each extension of the railway was worked by the Highland Railway, which subscribed to the funds of the local companies, save the Duke of Sutherland's Railway, which was entirely a private venture. However, with the exception of the Ross-shire Railway, which by its amalgamation with the Inverness & Aberdeen Junction Railway became part of the Highland Railway in 1865, the remaining four nominally retained their independence for a number of years.

The Dingwall & Skye Railway was merged on August 2nd, 1880, but it was not until July 28th, 1884, that the northern lines lost their identity. The new mileage added to the Highland Railway in these two years was as follows:

Dingwall & Skye Railway	53	miles
Sutherland Railway	26½	,,
Duke of Sutherland's Railway ...	17¼	,,
Sutherland & Caithness Railway ...	67¾	,,
Total	164½	miles

The year 1884 is one of the most important in the history of the Company, because the Act of that year consolidated the system almost into its complete form. With one highly important exception, the subsequent additions were in the nature of branch lines, most of them fairly short, which acted as feeders to the main routes. Save for two nominally-independent light railways, the whole of the lines built after 1884 were authorized as part of the Highland Railway, and not as separate undertakings to be amalgamated at a later date.

CHAPTER FIVE

EXPANSION 1884-1903

THE DIRECT LINE TO INVERNESS

OF THE additions made to the Highland Railway subsequent to 1884 by far the most important was that which shortened the main line from Inverness to the south. Although the route via Forres was a great improvement on that via Aberdeen, which it superseded, it was by no means as direct as could be desired. Leaving Inverness, it ran almost due east for 24 miles before turning to the south. In consequence, the village of Aviemore, in Strathspey, was over 60 miles by rail from Inverness, whereas the distance measured in a straight line was little more than 30 miles.

Despite this disadvantage, the promoters of the Inverness & Perth Junction Railway had good reasons for choosing the route that they did. Forres is situated almost midway between Inverness and Keith, and it was their intention to leave the Inverness & Aberdeen Junction Railway at the most central point possible, so that no place should be unduly side-tracked. Had a direct line been made to Inverness from Aviemore, or even from Grantown, it would have placed the whole of the Inverness & Aberdeen Junction Railway virtually on a branch line. Although Inverness itself would have benefited, passengers from places farther to the east would have had to make a considerable detour to reach the main line.

Nevertheless, it was realized at an early date that eventually steps would have to be taken to provide a shorter route to Inverness. For many years, however, the Highland Railway made no definite progress towards this. The country lying between Loch Ness and the Spey is composed of moorland, mostly well above sea level, with the Monadhliadh Mountains in the south-east. The whole district is wild, and much of it uninhabited. The building of a railway through such country would have been a costly undertaking, with almost negligible prospects of an adequate return from local traffic. In addition, the shortening of the route would have necessitated a substantial reduction in the rates for through traffic to Inverness.

Finally, the Company's hand was forced by a threat of an independent and shorter route to Inverness from the south, promoted in close association with the North British Railway (see Chapter Six). Powers were obtained on July 28th, 1884, for a new line leaving the existing route at Aviemore, and passing through Carr Bridge and Moy to Inverness. On May 23rd, 1887, an Act authorizing a deviation near Inverness was obtained, and a third Act, dated June 27th, 1892, again slightly altered the location of the railway. The first section, from Aviemore to Carr Bridge, 6¾ miles, was opened on July 8th, 1892; the 17 miles to Daviot followed on July 19th, 1897; and the final 11 miles to Inverness were completed on November 1st, 1898.

The engineering works were exceptionally heavy, and included two large viaducts over the rivers Findhorn and Nairn. The former, 445 yds long, and constructed on a curve of half a mile radius, consisted of nine steel spans, supported on masonry columns, with a maximum height of 143 ft; and the Nairn viaduct, 600 yds long, and built entirely of red sandstone, was composed of 28 arches of 50 ft span, and one span of 100 ft over the river. The maximum height was 128 ft. Near Slochd Mhuic Summit, where the line reached a height of 1,315 ft above sea level, were two deep cuttings and a masonry viaduct of eight arches, over 100 ft high. The ascent to the summit from Inverness was severe, including several miles at 1 in 60, or little easier. The rise from Aviemore, although shorter, was almost as hard.

When the works were nearing completion, the Highland Railway was robbed by death of one of its oldest officers, Murdoch Paterson, the chief engineer. Paterson had been in the service of the Company since its earliest days, and had held the position of chief engineer since 1875. He died in the house provided for the stationmaster at Culloden Moor,* whither he had gone to superintend the building of the Nairn viaduct. Paterson was succeeded by his resident engineer, William Roberts, who held office until 1914, being succeeded in his turn by Alexander Newlands.

The distance from Perth to Inverness via the new line was 118 miles, as against 144 via Forres. A substantial reduction in journey times was at once secured. The principal trains were diverted to the Carr Bridge line, and the older route became a secondary main line.

OTHER NEW LINES

With a view to participating in the lucrative fishing trade of the towns of Buckie and Portessie, and to tap the farming district lying between Keith and the coast, known as the Enzie, the Highland Railway obtained powers, on July 12th, 1882, to construct a branch from Keith to a junction with the Portsoy–Elgin line of the Great North of Scotland Railway (authorized on the same day) at Portessie, a distance of 13¾ miles. The two railways ran parallel for some distance between Buckie and Portessie, and at the latter town the Highland Railway used the GNSR station. The line was opened on August 1st, 1884.

The railway remained in use until August 9th, 1915. Subsequently the track was removed between Aultmore (near Keith) and Buckie, and used elsewhere. No buildings were demolished, as it was intended to re-open the line after the war. Restoration of the permanent way was delayed because for many years the traffic had been light, and it was not considered expedient to re-open the branch for the time being. It was still closed when the Highland Railway became part of the LMSR in 1923.

With the growth in popularity of Strathpeffer as a spa, the

*When the new line was opened, Culloden station on the original Inverness & Nairn Railway was renamed Allanfearn.

need for better railway facilities became apparent, as the station on the Dingwall & Skye Railway, known as Strathpeffer, was about 1½ miles from the village, at the top of a steep hill. In the early 1880s representations were made to the Highland Railway, with a view to the construction of a branch from Dingwall to a centrally-situated terminus.

Powers for the new railway were obtained on July 28th, 1884, and the line was opened on June 3rd of the next year. From Dingwall, the older line was followed for 2¼ miles to Fodderty Junction, where the Dingwall & Skye Railway turned sharply towards the hills, to begin its long climb to Raven Rock Summit. The branch kept to the lower ground, and reached its terminus after a further run of 2½ miles. On the opening of the new line the existing station was renamed Achterneed.

On July 4th, 1890, powers were obtained to extend the Burghead branch to the fishing village of Hopeman, a distance of 2 miles. The extension diverged from the original branch at a point a little to the south of the terminus. A new passenger station, at the eastern end of the town, was provided to serve Burghead.

The extension was opened on October 10th, 1892. On that date the old terminus was closed for passenger traffic, but goods trains continued over the line to serve Burghead pier. About half a mile from Hopeman the railway passed near to the large stone quarries of Cummingston. A station was opened at this point, on October 1st, 1892, but it was closed on April 1st, 1904.

Some 8 miles east of Elgin lies the small town of Fochabers-on-Spey. When the Inverness & Aberdeen Junction Railway was opened to Keith, the second station east from Elgin was named Fochabers. This was, however, a decided misnomer, because the town was some 4 miles distant, along an indirect road.

Five years later, on June 8th, 1863, a nominally-independent company, the Fochabers & Garmouth, obtained an Act for a line from Fochabers station to Garmouth, passing some distance to the west of the town. The scheme was virtually a resuscitation of one of the branches included in the ambitious programme of the Great North of Scotland Railway in 1846. Both the Inverness & Aberdeen Junction and the Inverness & Perth Junction companies were empowered to subscribe towards the construction of the railway, and the former undertook to work it. The necessary capital was not forthcoming, and the powers lapsed before any construction could be undertaken.

When the Great North of Scotland Railway opened its line from Keith to Elgin, via the coast, a station named Fochabers was provided on the east bank of the Spey, opposite Garmouth. Here again the name was misleading, as the distance from the town was about 4 miles, and Fochabers acquired the doubtful distinction of possessing two of the most inconveniently-situated stations in the country.

On June 27th, 1892, the Highland Railway obtained powers for a branch, 3 miles long, from Fochabers station to a point on the west bank of the Spey, about half a mile from the town. The Spey is very wide here, and to avoid a costly bridge, the railway was not carried over the river. The branch was opened on October 16th, 1893, on which date the original Fochabers station was renamed Orbliston Junction. To avoid confusion with the GNSR station, the terminus of the new line was renamed Fochabers Town on July 1st, 1894. The GNSR station was renamed Spey Bay in 1918.

The peninsula lying between the Beauly and Cromarty Firths is known as the Black Isle. The district boasts much rich farm land, while on the south coast is Fortrose, a thriving fishing centre. Owing to its peculiar geographical position the isle is somewhat isolated, and was not placed on the main railway route to the north. The nearest point on the Highland Railway's main line was Muir of Ord, some 13 miles from Fortrose.

To tap this district, and to provide transport for the fishing industry, powers were obtained on July 4th, 1890, for a branch line on the south side of the isle, from Muir of Ord to

Rosemarkie, a distance of 15¾ miles. On February 1st, 1894, the railway was opened as far as Fortrose, but the extension to Rosemarkie was never begun. The journey to Inverness was indirect, but short of a costly bridge over the Beauly Firth at Kessock Ferry, a better route could not be secured.

Strome Ferry, the original western terminus of the Dingwall & Skye Railway, is not an ideal place for a pier. Loch Carron is subject to strong currents and it is frequently difficult to bring a ship alongside. The extension of the railway to Kyle of Lochalsh was often suggested, but for many years nothing was done. At length it became clear that Strome Ferry was in danger of losing its monopoly of the traffic to the Isle of Skye and the Outer Hebrides. The West Highland Railway had been authorized in 1889 from a junction with the North British Railway at Craigendoran (24 miles from Glasgow) to Fort William, and there was every possibility that the Company would soon seek powers to extend the line westwards to the Sound of Sleat. The establishment of a new port in this vicinity would have robbed Strome Ferry of much of its trade, as quite apart from the difficult approach to the pier, the railway journey to the south, via Inverness, was somewhat roundabout.

On June 29th, 1893, the Highland Railway obtained powers to extend the railway from Strome Ferry to Kyle of Lochalsh, and to provide a pier there. The engineering works were heavy, as the line wound in and out along the shore through a series of deep rock cuttings. The site for the station at Kyle had to be blasted out of the solid rock.

The extension was opened on November 2nd, 1897, on which date the old pier at Strome Ferry was closed, and the ships transferred to Kyle of Lochalsh. Between Strome Ferry and Plockton a private station to serve Duncraig Castle was provided. There were intermediate stations for public traffic at Plockton and Duirinish.

Powers for the West Highland Extension Railway from Fort William to Mallaig had been obtained on July 31st, 1894, and the competitive port, situated 22 miles south of Kyle of

Lochalsh, was opened in 1901. Although a considerable share of the Hebridean traffic passed into the hands of the North British Railway, the Highland Railway retained the valuable mail contract, as well as the monopoly of traffic destined for Inverness and the north-east of Scotland.

The original line from Inverness to Nairn had provided a station to serve the military post of Fort George. This was only Fort George in name, as the depot itself was some $3\frac{1}{2}$ miles to the north, at the end of a sandy tongue of land jutting out into the Moray Firth. It was felt that the fort should be made more accessible by rail, and powers were granted on July 4th, 1890, for the construction of a branch, $1\frac{1}{2}$ miles long, from the existing Fort George station to the village of Ardersier, which lies some 2 miles south of the depot proper. The terminus of the new line was to be called Fort George.

The surrounding country is level and sandy, and no difficulties were experienced in the construction of the line, which was opened for traffic on July 1st, 1899. The junction station was renamed Gollanfield Junction, from the farm of the same name in the neighbourhood.

As has been mentioned already, the county town of Dornoch was left some 7 miles from the railway, the connexion being supplied by a coach which plied to and from the railway station at The Mound. This means of conveyance was inconvenient, and towards the end of the century the desire to obtain better railway communication began to grow in the district.

The Highland Railway was in favour of the scheme, and on August 13th, 1898, an order was obtained for a standard-gauge light railway, $7\frac{3}{4}$ miles long, leaving the Highland Railway at The Mound, and following the coach road closely. Although the Highland Railway agreed to work the line, the local Company remained nominally independent until the grouping.

The railway was opened for traffic on June 2nd, 1902. Although theoretically a light railway, the line was substantially built, and differed but little from the main line. The Board of Trade imposed many restrictions, which resulted in a much heavier expenditure than would otherwise have been necessary. Unlike many light railways, the line was fenced throughout, and gates were provided at the numerous level crossings. But the permanent way was lighter than that on the main line, and the rails were spiked direct to the sleepers.

Although Dornoch was reached from the south by a very circuitous route, the light railway was a great benefit to the town. It was possible to complete the journey without change of carriage, but such facilities were only provided for one summer, some years after the railway was opened (see Chapter Nine).

Wick and Lybster Light Railway Company.

OPENING OF LINE,
1st JULY 1903.

LUNCHEON AT LYBSTER AT 1.30.

Admit _Mr Duff Dunbar_

J K Smith *Secy.*

NOT TRANSFERABLE.

The indirect course adopted by the Sutherland & Caithness Railway between Wick and Helmsdale deprived the coastal villages lying to the south of the Caithness fishing port of a railway for many years. With high-speed mechanical road transport still a dream of the future, this was a serious disadvantage to places where inhabitants depended for their livelihood on the quick disposal of such a perishable commodity as fish.

On November 27th, 1899, powers were obtained for a light railway, 13¾ miles long, from Wick to Lybster. A Treasury grant of £25,000 was obtained, and the remaining capital was subscribed partly by the Highland Railway and partly by local subscription. The chief shareholders were the Caithness County Council and the Duke of Portland, who owned large estates in the neighbourhood. The total capital subscribed was £72,000.

The contractor for building the line was William Kennedy, of Glasgow. No special difficulties were encountered, and the railway was opened on July 1st, 1903. The Highland Railway undertook to work the line at cost price. In many respects the undertaking was similar to the Dornoch Light Railway. The rails were spiked direct to the sleepers, the line was fenced

From	To	Mls	Chs	
Stanley	Inverness station	110	60	via Carr Bridge
Aviemore	Inverness, Rose Street	60	43	via Forres and Inverness Loop
Inverness station	Wick	161	16	
Forres	Keith	30	20	
Dingwall	Kyle of Lochalsh	63	50	
Keith	Portessie	13	71	
Muir of Ord	Fortrose	13	45	
Ballinluig	Aberfeldy	8	59	
Alves	Hopeman	7	37*	
Georgemas	Thurso	6	52	
Orbliston Junction	Fochabers Town	3	00	
Fodderty Junction	Strathpeffer	2	38	
Gollanfield Junction	Fort George	1	38	
Inverness Harbour branch		0	69	
Muirtown Basin branch†		0	58	
Wick & Lybster Light Railway‡		13	44	
Dornoch Light Railway‡		7	51	
Total		506	31	

*Including Burghead Pier Branch, 32 chs.

†Goods traffic only.

‡Nominally independent lines worked by the Highland until Grouping.

Invergarry & Fort Augustus Railway, worked by the Highland from July 1903 to April 1907 – 24 mls 16 chs.

throughout, and gates were provided at most of the numerous level crossings.

Although the route to the south was by no means direct, the line was of great service to the district through which it passed, and the fishing industry reaped the benefit, especially at Lybster, where the Duke of Portland spent large sums on improvements to the harbour.

THE EXTENT OF THE SYSTEM

The opening of the Wick & Lybster Light Railway marks the limit of growth of the Highland Railway. In the 18 years following, during which the Company maintained its separate existence, no new lines were opened. The system was now complete, and was made up as shown in the table on page 45.

CHAPTER SIX

THE INVERGARRY & FORT AUGUSTUS RAILWAY

THREAT FROM THE NORTH BRITISH

IN SOME remote, prehistoric age, a great earth-movement took place in what is now the North of Scotland, and the land was split by an immense rift running across the country from north-east to south-west. Subsequently, there was formed in this hollow a chain of lochs whence rivers flowed to the North Sea or the Atlantic.

Coming to historical times, we find at the north end of the rift the Highland capital, Inverness, and at the other, the one-time military post of Fort William. The rift, or Great Glen, as it is usually called, has always been a natural highway across the country.

Early in the nineteenth century, the chain of lochs was connected by means of canals to afford a waterway for the passage of ships. Unfortunately, the shallowness of the canals and the cramped dimensions of the locks imposed drastic limitations on the size of the ships passing through, and the undertaking never justified the enormous expense of its con-struction. The canal is still used by trawlers passing between the east and west coast fishing grounds, but regular passenger services have been withdrawn.

For many years the water and roadways through the glen remained unchallenged by the railway. At length, when a line was suggested, the proposal came not, as might have been expected, from the Highland Railway, but from the North British Railway, the bulk of whose system was in the densely-populated industrial area of the Lowlands. To understand how this Company came to penetrate into a district so far removed from the scene of its main activities, it is necessary to consider briefly certain aspects of its early history and development.

In 1842, railway communication was established between Edinburgh and Glasgow. Sixteen years later, a separate company made an extension along the north bank of the Clyde to Helensburgh, some 25 miles from the city. The Helensburgh Railway was absorbed by its larger neighbour in 1862. Four years later the Edinburgh & Glasgow and North British Railways were amalgamated. North of the Firth of Clyde the country becomes wild and mountainous, and many years elapsed before an attempt was made to carry a railway through this district.

In 1884, an independent company, under the title of the Glasgow & North Western Railway, was formed to build a line from the North British Railway at Maryhill (in the northern suburbs of Glasgow), through Strathblane and Drymen, to the eastern side of Loch Lomond. From the head of the loch, the railway was to pass through Crianlarich and Tyndrum, and thence by way of Rannoch Moor and the Pass of Glencoe to Loch Leven. That loch was to be crossed at its narrowest point, near Ballachulish, and the line then followed the coast, through Onich, to Fort William. It was also proposed to extend the railway through the Great Glen to Inverness, to join the Highland Railway. The total length of the undertaking was about 155 miles, and the distance from Glasgow to Inverness would have been about 160 miles. The distance by the Caledonian and Highland Railway was 207 miles.

Although the Company was nominally independent, it was backed by the North British. The Highland Railway realized that not only was it in danger of losing traffic, but it would also have to lower charges. Even had the threatened competition been countered by the shortened main line from Aviemore, the Highland Railway would still have been at a disadvantage by some 20 miles.

When the bill came before Parliament, the Highland Railway submitted that there was only traffic in paying quantities for one railway to the Northern Highlands. If the new route was constructed, it would lose valuable revenue, and this loss would prove an effectual barrier to further extensions of its own system in other directions. This argument was convincing enough to secure the rejection of the proposed new line, for the time being.

Some three years later the project was revived, under the title of the West Highland Railway, for a line from the North British Railway at Helensburgh to Fort William, via Loch Lomond, Rannoch Moor, and Spean Bridge. The branch through the Great Glen to Inverness was not included. The NBR was to work the line. For the moment there was no threat to Inverness, but the Highland opposed the bill. This time its efforts were unavailing, and the Act was passed in 1889. The railway was opened in 1894.

In 1893 two schemes were put forward for the connecting link to Inverness. The first was proposed by the Highland Railway, which naturally desired to control any line in the Great Glen. No sooner was this project in the field than a rival appeared, promoted by the West Highland Railway. After a great deal of argument, the two companies agreed to abandon the idea and the bills were withdrawn.

Two years later the West Highland and North British Railways brought forward a bill to extend the railway from Fort William to Mallaig, on the Sound of Sleat, a distance of 41 miles. The Highland Railway opposed the measure, because it would deflect the traffic from Strome Ferry, and the recently-sanctioned extension to Kyle of Lochalsh. Ultimately it was induced to withdraw its objection, and the bill passed. The West Highland and the North British Railways agreed not to promote directly, or indirectly, any railway through the Great Glen for at least ten years. The Highland Railway received £500 for its Parliamentary expenses.

A short time later, a local company, under the title of the Invergarry & Fort Augustus Railway, was floated to build a railway from Spean Bridge, on the West Highland Railway, to Fort Augustus, at the south end of Loch Ness, a distance of

24 miles. This proposal left a gap of about 30 miles between Fort Augustus and Inverness. After much opposition, the Act for the line was passed on August 14th, 1896.

It soon became evident that both the Highland and the North British companies considered that the authorization of the railway from Spean Bridge to Fort Augustus had cancelled the agreement of 1895, for in 1897 three schemes were launched for the connecting link between Fort Augustus and Inverness. The first was for an extension of the Invergarry Company's line, and the other two were put forward by the West Highland and the Highland Railways respectively. These latter sought to obtain running powers over the already-sanctioned portion of the Invergarry Railway. A fierce Parliamentary contest ensued. The Highland was anxious, at all costs, to keep its rivals out of Inverness; and the West Highland and North British Railways were desirous of keeping Fort William a close preserve. After a great deal of costly litigation, the preamble to the Highland Railway's bill was proved by the Commons, but the measure was thrown out by the Lords.

THE ISOLATED BRANCH

The local Company was therefore left to go ahead with the line from Spean Bridge to Fort Augustus. The works were completed towards the end of 1901, but then a fresh trouble arose. The construction of the line had been very costly. The number of culverts required to carry off mountain streams was enormous, and the earth works were heavy. The Company exhausted its funds in building the track, and had no money left for the purchase of rolling stock.

As the railway made physical connexion with the West Highland at Spean Bridge, the North British was approached with a view to working the line. That Company declared itself willing to do so at cost price – a good offer, considering that traffic would be light. However, the directors of the Invergarry Company demanded a guarantee of personal indemnity.

When this was refused, they offered their railway to the Highland.

This action aroused a fresh Parliamentary storm, every whit as fierce as that which had raged in 1897. Both the Highland and the North British were anxious to obtain control of the Invergarry line to the exclusion of the other. The result was that the opening of the line was delayed for some months. Finally, under the Act of June 30th, 1903, the Highland Railway was empowered to enter into an agreement to work the line for an annual payment of £4,000. At the same time it gave the North British a guarantee that it would never try to penetrate nearer to Fort William. The latter Company gave a similar promise with regard to Inverness. These undertakings practically destroyed all hope of the connecting link from Fort Augustus to Inverness being built. The railway was opened on July 22nd.

Under the agreement of 1903, the Highland Railway was to work the line for ten years, with the option of renewal. But traffic did not come up to expectations, and the line was entirely separated from the rest of its system. On May 1st, 1907, it withdrew in favour of the North British, which worked the railway for the next four years. At length, on October 31st, 1911, the services were completely suspended, at the instigation of the local Company. After remaining closed for almost two years, the line was reopened on August 1st, 1913, and again worked by the North British Railway, which in the ensuing year purchased the undertaking for £27,000.

Originally, the railway extended about three-quarters of a mile beyond Fort Augustus village to a pier on Loch Ness, at which steamers called. This extension included a hand-operated swing-bridge over the Caledonian Canal, and a viaduct over the River Oich. Until 1906 certain trains ran forward to the pier, during the summer only, but from October 1st of that year the service was suspended, and the line fell into decay. But some goods traffic continued until July 1924 after which most of the rails were removed, and the swing-bridge was kept permanently open for the passage of ships. The station buildings at the pier were demolished, and the boats ceased to call.

In 1905, while still working the Invergarry Railway, the Highland Railway applied for powers to own and operate steamships on Loch Ness. It was proposed that these ships should run in connexion with the trains, and supplement the existing service on the canal between Fort Augustus and Inverness.

The bill was strongly and successfully opposed by David MacBrayne, whose steamers held a monopoly on the northern part of the canal. Objections were also raised by the Invergarry Railway, which maintained that the establishment of such a steamer service would effectually enable the Highland Railway to block any attempt to complete the railway through the Great Glen.

Eventually, disaster once more overtook this waif of the railway world. Merged into the London & North Eastern Railway under the Railways Act of 1921, the line was worked by that Company for several years. At length, traffic fell to such an extent that it was decided to suspend the passenger services from December 1st, 1933. Arrangements were made for passengers and light goods traffic to be carried by road, but one coal train was scheduled on Saturdays. After the end of the Second World War, this occasional use of the railway was no longer justified. All traffic ceased from January 1st, 1947, and the dismantling of the track followed.

Such is the chequered and stormy history of this little railway, a history that is probably without parallel in railway annals. It is greatly to be deplored that saner counsels did not prevail in 1897, which might have led to the railway being completed to Inverness, and placed in the hands of a joint committee. Admittedly, the Highland Railway would have had to lower its rates to Inverness, but the new route would, doubtless, have brought additional traffic to other parts of the system. The prospects of the Invergarry Company would have been far brighter, and the line might well have become a paying concern, instead of a dead loss to its promoters.

CHAPTER SEVEN

SOME SCHEMES THAT FAILED

ULLAPOOL AND GAIRLOCH

DESPITE a sparse population, and relatively limited resources, the Highlands of Scotland have received their full share of attention from the railway promoter, and in addition to the existing lines a number of schemes have been mooted which have failed to materialize. Most belong to the decade between 1890 and 1900, although some of them come within the present century. Many of the proposed railways, although nominally independent, were backed by the Great North of Scotland Railway, in its attempts to secure an entry into Inverness. On the other hand, some were put forward, without the spur of competition, by the Highland Railway, or by an independent company.

The coasts of Wester Ross and Sutherland, although boasting no big towns, have in addition to Kyle of Lochalsh some harbours which might be developed as centres for the fishing industry. There are also certain other places that enjoy considerable favour as tourist resorts in the summer months. Chief among these is Ullapool, situated on sheltered Loch Broom. Established in 1788 by the British Fishery Society, as a base for the west-coast herring fishery, the village decayed with the decline of its industry. For many years there was a hope that it would be adopted as a Naval base, for which its land-locked harbour is well adapted. There was also the possibility that the fishing would revive, given adequate means of transport to the markets of the south.

Ullapool is the nearest port on the mainland for the Isle of Lewis. Indeed, at one time a steamer plied regularly to Stornoway. A direct road connects Loch Broom with Garve, on the Dingwall & Skye Railway, 32 miles distant.

With the possibility of securing a great increase of trade, it was deemed feasible, about the year 1890, to construct a railway to the village, and on August 14th of that year the Garve & Ullapool Railway was authorized. It was arranged that the Highland Railway should work the line, which would virtually become part of that system. The Company was unable to raise the necessary capital, and the scheme was shelved.

Two years later the Great North of Scotland Railway sought to obtain running powers over the Highland Railway from Elgin to Garve, and to work the Ullapool Railway. The Highland secured the defeat of this scheme, but no further progress was made with the original proposal, and the powers of the Company ultimately lapsed.

At Achnasheen, some distance west of Garve, there is another road from the railway to the west coast, serving the districts of Gairloch, Poolewe and Aultbea. In 1893, a railway, some 35 miles long, was proposed from Achnasheen to Aultbea. Once again, the Great North was behind the bill, and proposed to work the line, and secure running powers over the Highland Railway from Elgin to Achnasheen. The bill was presented and rejected in the 1893 session of Parliament.

In 1897 the Highland Railway came forward with a big programme for new lines, totalling 247 miles in all. The Ullapool and Gairloch schemes were revived, and two additional routes to the west coast were proposed. The first of these left the main line at Culrain, 60 miles north of Inverness, and keeping to the south bank of the River Oykell, ran by way of Rosehall and Oykell Bridge to the head waters of the river. Passing over the hills to Aultnacaelgach the Kirkaig River was followed to the west coast, whence the railway turned northwards to terminate at Lochinver, a total distance of 41 miles from Culrain.

Lochinver, with its fine land-locked bay, forms a good harbour, convenient for the Outer Hebrides. There were hopes that with the coming of the railway a port of call for ships serving the islands would be established. As is the case with

Ullapool and Gairloch, the district is rich in natural beauty and the trout-fishing is good.

The second route to the west left the main line at Lairg, and went by way of Loch Shin and Loch More to the coast at Loch Laxford, a distance of 42 miles. In common with all the other proposed lines, it suffered from the disadvantage of crossing a tract of country that, for the most part, consists of barren moorland, sparsely inhabited and unproductive, where local traffic would have been of the scantiest.

Despite great efforts by the local landowners, neither of these schemes ever came to fruition. It is difficult to see what hopes the promoters had of securing an adequate return for their money. True, the west coast attracts a large number of tourists and, doubtless, the railway would have increased this traffic. Beyond this, however, the source of revenue would have been meagre, although it is possible that a new fishing port might have been established at some point along the coast.

NORTH AND EAST COASTS

In addition to the routes to the west coast, there were proposals for new railways in the north of Sutherland and Caithness. In 1896 the Duke of Sutherland and certain other landowners formed themselves into a company for the construction of a standard-gauge light railway from Forsinard station, on the Highland Railway's northern main line, down Strath Halladale to Melvich and Port Skerra, a distance of about 14 miles. A pier was to be built at the northern terminus at which coasting steamers were to call.

Powers for the construction of the railway were obtained under the Forsinard Melvich & Port Skerra Light Railway Order of July 13th, 1898. Certain materials and plant for the construction of the line were taken to Forsinard station by the Highland Railway, which was to have built and worked the line, but construction was not started and powers for the line ultimately lapsed.

Dunnet Head

Gills Bay

Duncansby Head

Scrabster
Dunnet Bay
Kyle of Tongue
Portskerra
Thurso
John O'Groats House
Bettyhill
Melvich
Georgemas
Wick
Forsinard
Lybster
Dunbeath
L.Shin
Helmsdale
Lairg
The Mound
Golspie
Culrain
Bonar Bridge
Dornoch
Tarbat Ness
Dornoch Firth
Portmahomack
Tain
Cromarty
Firth
Fearn
Cromarty
Moray Firth
Dingwall
Forres
Fortrose
Conon
Nairn
Muir of Ord
R.Nairn
INVERNESS
Lochend
Loch Ness

5   0   5   10   15   20 MILES

Proposed Railways ‑ ‑ ‑ ‑ ‑
Railways actually built ━━━━━

The Highland Railway also proposed to extend its Thurso branch along the coast for 17 miles to Dunnet and Gills Bay. Farther to the south, there was to be a light railway from Wick to Lybster (13 miles), with a possible extension of 7 miles, to Dunbeath, to link up several fishing villages with the main line. The light railway from The Mound to Dornoch was also included in this programme. The line from Thurso to Gills Bay never materialized, but, as has been seen, the Lybster and Dornoch lines were built. The suggested extension from Lybster to Dunbeath was ultimately abandoned.

Certain outlying parts of Easter Ross were to be connected with the Highland Railway by means of light railways. One proposal was for a line from Fearn (near Tain) to Portmahomack on the southern shore of the Dornoch Firth, a distance of 9 miles. A great deal of discussion took place as to whether the railway should come right into Tain or not, with the result that no definite steps were taken for many years. Ultimately the scheme fell into abeyance.

By far the most interesting of the proposed lines is the light railway that was to have connected the town of Cromarty with the main line. Cromarty is situated on the north coast of the Black Isle, on the shores of the firth of the same name. A railway had already been built from Muir of Ord to Fortrose, but the line served the southern coast of the Isle, leaving the northern portion somewhat off the beaten track. It was to remedy this that the light railway was proposed in 1897.

The original scheme was for a line from Cromarty to Dingwall, the county town. The Conon River was to be crossed at Alcaig Ferry, by a bridge of considerable size. A fierce discussion raged for a long time amongst those interested as to whether the proposed route was the best. It was felt in certain quarters that the railway should not include the expensive bridge at Alcaig, but should join the Highland Railway at Conon, to the south of Dingwall. Equally strong was the opinion that the line would be at a disadvantage if this route were adopted, and that the terminus should be at the county town.

The Light Railway Commission refused all assistance if the direct route to Dingwall was adopted, since it considered the bridge at Alcaig unnecessary. Ultimately, the Conon route was adopted. A further delay occurred at once while the promoters were trying to come to terms with the Highland Railway, so that the trains could run forward from Conon to Dingwall. This matter was still undecided when the Order was obtained on August 1st, 1902.

Some time elapsed before construction was begun. Eventually a start was made, not, as might have been expected, from the junction at Conon, but from Cromarty. Considerable difficulty in the acquisition of certain lands led to this plan being adopted. Progress was by no means rapid, and Extension of Time Orders were obtained on November 4th, 1907, and April 7th, 1910. By 1914 the track had been laid for about 6 miles, at the side of the main road from Cromarty, and the works, including a substantial bridge at Cullicudden Farm, were well in hand for a further 2 miles. The remaining 11 miles had not been started.

On the outbreak of the First World War, all work was suspended, and about a year later the track was taken up and used elsewhere. Subsequently, nothing was done towards reinstating or completing the line, and the works lay derelict. The course of the abandoned cuttings and embankments remain clearly to be seen. In addition to the bridge at Cullicudden, which was built in concrete, several other small bridges and culverts had been constructed, but no permanent buildings had been erected. It is strange that the line should have been allowed to lie derelict in this way after so much money had been spent, particularly as the district served is far richer than is the case with most of the other lines previously mentioned.

SKYE AND LEWIS

The remainder of the Highland Railway's programme for 1897 comprised proposals for light railways in the islands of

Skye and Lewis. For some years there had been much vague talk of providing the larger Hebridean Islands with railway facilities, but the proposals had never taken concrete shape. At length, the approaching completion of the railway from Strome Ferry to Kyle of Lochalsh led the various landowners to come to the Highland Railway with definite schemes.

On the Isle of Skye, one terminus of the proposed railway was to be at Kyle Akin, situated immediately opposite to the new pier at Kyle of Lochalsh, and separated from the mainland by a narrow strait, less than half a mile wide. Thence the line was to run by way of Broadford to Torrin, on Loch Slapin, on the west coast. The total length of the railway was $14\frac{1}{2}$ miles.

In Lewis, the railway was to run from Stornoway, the chief town, westwards to Breasclet, and thence slightly north to Carloway, on the west coast, a distance of 21 miles.

Early in 1897 a party of Highland Railway officers crossed over to both islands, and went over the ground with the local landowners. In each case it was proposed to obtain an order under the Light Railways Act, and to apply for a Government grant. The Highland Railway was asked to subscribe a certain amount of the capital, and to build and work the lines. The remainder of the money was to be raised by local subscription. After a lengthy discussion the Highland directors decided not to proceed further with the scheme, as in their opinion there was not enough traffic for the railways to pay. Both schemes fell into abeyance.

In the following year a London syndicate, known as the Hebridean Light Railway Company, was formed. The support of the North British Railway was sought, as that Company was to work the West Highland Extension Railway, from Fort William to Mallaig, at that time under construction. A fresh terminus was selected in Skye, at Isle Ornsay, on the Sound of Sleat, whence it is an easy crossing of about 10 miles to Mallaig.

Surveys were made for a railway from Isle Ornsay through Broadford and Sligachan to Portree, whence the line crossed the island to terminate at Uig, on Loch Snizort, where there is

Proposed railways in the Isle of Skye

a large fish-curing station. A branch of the railway was to run from Portree to Bernisdale and Dunvegan.

In Lewis it was proposed to build a railway from Stornoway to Tarbert (Harris), and from Stornoway to Carloway and Dunan Pier (on Loch Carloway), with a branch to Breasclet. The total length of these proposals was about 130 miles, of which rather more than one-half was in Skye.

On April 23rd, 1898, the Company gave notice that it proposed to make application under the Light Railways Act for powers to construct all of the above lines, except that from Stornoway to Tarbert. The gauge of the railways was to be 3 ft 6 ins, and the estimated cost was £500,000. It was proposed to apply for a grant of £150,000, and for a loan of £60,000, from the Government. The remainder of the capital was to be raised by subscription.

In the Hebrides the proposals met with a very mixed reception. In certain quarters they were hailed as the salvation of the islands. On the other hand, grave doubts were expressed as to whether the crofters were in a position to carry the burden of the increased rates that would have had to be imposed. Many people, while admitting the usefulness of the railways, were convinced that they could never pay. Dissatisfaction was expressed because the lines in Skye did not run to Kyle Akin, to link up with the Highland Railway. It was feared that the coasting steamers would cease to run after the railways had been built, and leave some places entirely without transport facilities. Finally, a certain section maintained that the steamers were providing adequate facilities, and that the railways were not required.

The upshot was that the necessary capital was not forthcoming, and in the long run this was just as well. It is highly improbable that the lines would ever have repaid the cost of construction. In addition, the schemes of 1898 were under the tutelage of the North British Railway, and any attempt to carry them out would have led to the most determined opposition on the part of the Highland Railway, and the west-coast shipping interests. Such a contest might easily have resulted in the unhappy history of the Invergarry & Fort Augustus Railway being repeated in the Hebrides.

LOCH NESS AND STANLEY–DUNDEE

In 1897 a company was floated to build a light railway from Inverness to the head of Loch Ness, a distance of about 8 miles. It was proposed that the new line should branch from the Highland Railway, a short distance west of Inverness station, cross the Caledonian Canal by a swing-bridge, and run by way of Dunain to Lochend. Although there was to be a junction with the Highland Railway, no arrangements had been made either for that Company to work the line, or for the trains to enter Inverness station. It was hoped, however, that running powers would be granted.

The promoters applied for an order under the Light Railways Act, and the Commissioners heard the case on May 23rd, 1899. It was urged for the Company that besides benefiting the district through which it would pass, the line would improve communications to Fort Augustus and Fort William. The chief opposition came from the Invergarry & Fort Augustus Railway, which claimed that the railway was only a 'blocking' line, and would prevent the completion of its undertaking to Inverness. This opposition, and the fact that no settlement had been reached about the use of Inverness station, brought about the rejection of the scheme. The idea was never revived.

From time to time the possibility of building a direct railway from Dundee to the Highland Railway at Stanley had been discussed, but no definite steps had ever resulted. In 1901, however, a route was surveyed. It was proposed to use the Caledonian station at Dundee, whence the line passed to the west, through the village of Balbeggie, to Stanley, a distance of about 15 miles. This represented a saving of some 12 miles over the route via Perth.

Early in 1902 a meeting was held in Dundee to discuss the

LEWIS

Broad Bay

Duran Pier
L. Carloway   Carloway
Loch Bernera   Breasclet   *Stornoway*
L. Roag

L. Erisort

HARRIS   Loch Sheil

W.L. Tarbert

Tarbert   Loch Seaforth

E.L. Tarbert

10   5   0   10   20

MILES

Proposed railways in the Isle of Lewis

proposal. Although the Highland Railway was represented, the Company made no definite promises, beyond agreeing to give the question of working the line full consideration at the appropriate time. It was, however, agreed that the promoters should go ahead with the scheme, and gain as much support as possible. The plans were given a great deal of publicity in the Press, certain journals waxing enthusiastic over the possibilities of the new line, both as regards the desirability of a much shortened route to the Highlands, and the opening up of a new district hitherto untouched by railways. But the eulogies were the only support that the promoters ever received. Financial assistance was conspicuous by its absence, and the scheme was dropped.

1918 AND AFTERWARDS

In February 1918 a committee was appointed by the Secretary of State for Scotland to consider and report on the rural areas of the country that were in most need of improved transport for the promotion of local industries. The committee considered not only schemes for extending and improving the railway system, but also went into the question of new roads and additional steamer services. As the result of its deliberations a number of proposals affecting the territory of the Highland Railway were made. Many of them were, however, only resuscitations of the Highland Railway's programme of 1897.

The schemes for railways to Lochinver, Ullapool, Gills Bay and Portmahomack were revived, as was the proposal to extend the Wick & Lybster Light Railway to Dunbeath. It was also proposed to relay and complete the Cromarty Railway. An entirely new proposal was for the extension of the Thurso branch to Scrabster harbour, a distance of 2 miles. The need for bridging this awkward gap in the short sea route to the Orkneys had become more than ever apparent with the outbreak of the First World War, when a constant stream of special heavy traffic began to pass to and from the Naval base at Scapa Flow. The committee also considered the possibility of constructing a narrow-gauge light railway, primarily intended for the carriage of timber, from Beauly to Invercannich, and of linking up the Highland and West Highland Railways by means of a new cross-country line from Newtonmore to Tulloch. The latter was by no means a new proposal. As far back as 1861, a preliminary survey had been made for a railway from Kingussie to Fort William by virtually the same route. Although the scheme proved abortive, it undoubtedly hastened the promotion of the Dingwall & Skye Railway.

The committee issued its report before the war had ended. After the cessation of hostilities it was not deemed advisable to embark on the construction of any new railways, although many of the committee's suggestions for new roads were subsequently carried out.

Although many attempts have been made to open up the more distant parts of the Scottish Highlands by means of railways, adverse economic conditions have proved an insurmountable barrier. Even while the horse still reigned supreme on the roads, it had become obvious that neither the Highland Railway nor an independent company could undertake the construction of railways in those thinly-populated and largely unproductive districts unless a very generous measure of State aid was guaranteed. And that is a step which the Treasury has never felt justified in taking.

CHAPTER EIGHT

ATTACKS FROM THE EAST

KEITH AND ELGIN

THE DISPUTES and friction with the Great North of Scotland Railway which characterized the early history of the Highland Railway were destined to continue and play a prominent part in the course of subsequent events. Relations between the two Companies continued strained; and the position was made much worse when the Highland secured its own route to the south. At a comparatively early date, steps were taken to extend the Great North from Keith to Elgin, but many years elapsed ere that Company began to cast covetous eyes on Inverness.

On July 27th, 1857, an independent company, the Keith & Dufftown, obtained its Act for a railway between those two towns. The Great North contributed towards the building of the line, which was opened on February 12th, 1862, and arranged to work it. The GNSR also helped to build, and worked, the Strathspey Railway, authorized May 17th, 1861, from Dufftown to Nethy Bridge, and opened on July 1st, 1863. A continuation of the railway beyond Nethy Bridge, authorized on July 5th, 1865, and opened on August 1st, 1866, joined the Highland Railway at Boat of Garten.

At Craigellachie, 4 miles from Dufftown, the Strathspey Railway joined the Morayshire Railway, whose history has already been noted. By means of these local lines the Great North gained an entry into Elgin on July 1st, 1863. The distance from Keith to Elgin, via Craigellachie, was 27½ miles, as against 18 by the Highland Railway's route.

The Great North's alternative route, via the coast, was made much later, although the first portion, from Grange to Portsoy, was authorized under the Banffshire Railway Act of June 27th, 1857, and opened on August 2nd, 1859. An extension from Portsoy to Buckie, authorized on July 21st, 1863, was abandoned by the Act of July 12th, 1867. One year previously (July 30th, 1866) the Banffshire Railway had been amalgamated with the Great North.

It was not until July 12th, 1882, that powers were obtained for the railway from Portsoy to Elgin.* This extension was

HIGHLAND RAILWAY COMPANY.

W. ⟨⟨⟨⟨

STAFF NOTICE.

Office of Superintendent of Line,
INVERNESS, 18th December 1886.

KEITH STATION.

The following are the working arrangements for the above:—

SIGNALS WROUGHT FROM INTERLOCKING CABIN.

1. The Down Distant Signal for Main Line, situated on right-side of Line, 1150 yards west of Cabin.

2. The Down Home Signal for Main Line, situated on same side, 150 yards west of Cabin.

3. The Distant Signal from Buckie Section, situated on left side of Line, 1150 yards west of Cabin.

4. The Home Signal from Buckie Section, situated on left side of Line, 150 yards west of Cabin.

5. The Signal for Trains from Keith for Mulben and Buckie is situated on left side of Line, 160 yards east of Cabin. (The top arm on Post controls Trains from Keith to Mulben, the middle arm controls Trains to Buckie Section, and the lower arm controls Trains from Goods Yard.)

6. The Signal to admit Up Trains from "Loop" Line to Main for Mulben is situated on left hand side, 54 yards west of Signal Cabin.

7. The Signal to admit from New Siding at back of Engine Shed to Up Main is situated at the Fouling Point thereof.

SIGNALS NOT WROUGHT FROM INTERLOCKING CABIN.

To admit to Passenger Station.—The Single Disc immediately west of Passenger Arcade.

For Exchange Trains between Highland and Great North of Scotland Companies.—Two single armed Semaphore Signals immediately west of Passenger Arcade.

The Exchange Signal admitting from Great North to Highland is interlocked with Signal Cabin, but under charge of Station-Master.

POINTS.

1. The Down Main Line Facing Points, situated 150 yards west of Cabin.

2. The Buckie Section Facing Points, situated 150 yards west of Cabin.

3. The Facing Points from Keith for Up Main Line, or for Buckie Section, situated 46 yards east of Cabin.

4. The Trailing Points from Buckie Section, situated 46 yards east of Cabin.

5. The Siding Points from Goods Yard for Up Main Line, or Buckie Section, situated 160 yards east of Cabin, and which are controlled by the lower arm on the Three Armed Signal Post, close by them.

6. The Crossover Points from Up to Down Main Line, or vice versa, situated 165 yards east of Cabin.

7. The Points from Up Main Line to new Siding at back of Engine Shed, and which are controlled by a small Siding Signal at Fouling Point.

ENGINE WHISTLES.

From Passenger Station for Main Line, and from Main Line for Passenger Station	1 Whistle.
From Passenger Station for Buckie Line, and from Buckie Line for Passenger Station	2 Whistles.
From Goods Yard for Main Line, and from Main Line for Goods Yard	3 do.
From Goods Yard for Buckie Line, and from Buckie Line for Goods Yard	4 do.
Exchange Trains between Highland and Great North of Scotland Companies	5 do.

Bell Communication between the Passenger Station and Interlocking Signal Cabin.

The Bell Beats for the respective Trains to be the same in all cases as the Engine Whistles; and must *in every instance be acknowledged by repetition.*

N.B.—The starting of all Trains—that is to say, both from Passenger and Goods Department—*is solely under the charge of the Passenger Station Master.*

Guards of all Trains from Goods Yard must intimate personally to the Passenger Station-Master when their Train is ready to start.

To come into operation on Monday, the 22nd current.

This cancels all previous notices with respect to the foregoing.

Please acknowledge receipt.

By order.

THOMAS ROBERTSON,
Superintendent of Line.

*The Highland Railway branch from Keith to Portessie was authorized on the same day.

bitterly opposed by the Highland, which succeeded in obtaining running powers between Buckie and Portsoy ($11\frac{1}{2}$ miles). In return for this facility, the Great North secured running powers over the Highland Railway between Elgin and Forres ($12\frac{1}{4}$ miles). It was, however, laid down that neither Company should exercise its powers if the other refrained from so doing. Since the Highland never attempted to run to Portsoy, the powers of the Great North were completely useless. The extension was opened in sections: from Portsoy to Tochieneal on April 1st, 1884; from Elgin to Garmouth on August 12th of the same year; and from Tochieneal to Garmouth on May 3rd, 1886.

For many years all traffic between the Highland and the Great North of Scotland Railways was exchanged at Keith, and no attempt was made to provide connexions at Elgin. In 1880, however, William Moffatt was appointed general manager of the Great North, and a vigorous policy of improvement and expansion was at once instituted. Previously the Company had never attempted to run any expresses, but it was not long before some quite creditable trains were provided between Aberdeen and Elgin, and representations were made to the Highland Railway with a view to expediting the service between Elgin and Inverness.

The Great North desired the exchange of traffic to take place at Elgin, so that it could secure the greater mileage, but the Highland opposed any alteration. For the time being, open warfare was avoided by means of 'Facility Clauses' in certain Acts, which still left Keith as the chief point of exchange, but the directors of the Great North were by no means satisfied, and determined to seek independent access to Inverness.

In 1884, a company was floated, under the title of the Strathspey, Strathdon & Deeside Junction Railway, to build a line from Ballater, the terminus of the Great North's Deeside branch, to Nethy Bridge, on that Company's Strathspey line. The route passed over the hills to Cock Bridge, in Strathdon, and thence through the village of Tomintoul, a distance of about 30 miles. The Great North supported the proposal, and at the same time came forward with a scheme for a line from Nethy Bridge to Inverness, via Carr Bridge. The distance from Aberdeen to Inverness by this route would have been about 115 miles. As has been seen, the Highland countered this proposal with a bill for its direct line from Aviemore to Inverness, which was successful. Both the schemes backed by the Great North were thrown out.

The opening of the railway from Portsoy to Elgin brought the question of the exchange of traffic at the latter town to a head. The new line served a number of prosperous fishing towns on the Banffshire coast, and it was desired to run through trains from Aberdeen to Inverness by this route. In the opinion of the Great North, the Highland would not offer sufficient facilities for exchanging the traffic at Elgin. In 1886, after much argument, the two companies entered into a seven-year agreement with regard to the through traffic, but this was by no means a success.

The dispute dragged on for years, and as frequently happens in this type of contest, it was the customers of the two railways who suffered the most. To them the outward signs of the struggle were a lamentable lack of facilities, both for passengers and goods, which frequently resulted in vexatious and costly delays. Both sides were high-handed and uncompromising. Added to this was the determination of the Great North to reach Inverness with its own trains.

The Great North was not satisfied with the traffic agreement, and in 1890 it applied for powers to build its own line from Elgin to Inverness. The proposed route ran more or less parallel to the existing Highland Railway, which was to be crossed in several places. A branch from Elgin to Burghead was included in the proposals, as were also running powers over the Highland Railway from Inverness to Muir of Ord, whence a branch was to run to Fortrose. The Highland was able to bring sufficient opposition to secure the defeat of all these schemes, but immediately afterwards obtained powers for the Black Isle branch and the extension from Burghead to Hopeman.

Foiled in its direct attempts to reach Inverness by means of an independent line, the Great North next tried to secure running powers over the Highland Railway from Elgin to Inverness. As has been noted already, it came forward in 1892 behind the revival of the Garve & Ullapool Railway, and again in the following year in support of the Achnasheen, Gairloch and Aultbea scheme (see Chapter 7). In both cases the Great North proposed to reach the new lines by means of running powers from Elgin. These powers would, of course, have included access to Inverness. Both schemes were defeated.

In 1893 the seven-year agreement with regard to the through traffic came to an end. The Highland at once made certain alterations in the through trains, alleging that there was not enough traffic for them to omit all the local stations between Inverness and Elgin. The Great North maintained that the Highland was not justified in making these changes. An appeal to the Railway Commissioners resulted in the drawing-up of a timetable, which was supposed to get rid of the difficulties, but the Great North was by no means satisfied.

In 1895 it applied for running powers over the Highland track from Elgin to Inverness. In the course of the evidence an interesting piece of railway history came to light, which might have had an important bearing on the case, but it was ruled out of court. It will be remembered that the original Great North of Scotland Railway Act of 1846 authorized a line from Aberdeen to Inverness, but this was only completed as far as Keith. When the Inverness & Nairn Railway was promoted, the Great North gave notice of opposition, on the grounds that it was an invasion of the territory assigned to it by Parliament. It was, however, induced to withdraw opposition by a promise of running powers between Inverness and Nairn when it had extended its line to Nairn. By some oversight this agreement was never included in the Act authorizing the railway. Counsel for the Great North urged that the agreement was still binding in 1895, but the point was not allowed.

The Great North complained that the Highland trains were

constantly unpunctual, and that delays occurred to its services at Elgin. It also alleged that the Highland would not take through coaches from the Craigellachie line, and only one set from the coast line. It contended that it had the right to run the through coaches by whichever route it pleased, and that it would be able to work the trains more punctually and expeditiously if it secured running powers.

The Highland Railway opposed on the grounds that there was not enough traffic for separate trains to be run, and that as the line was single, delays were liable to occur if more trains were run. Opposition also came from the town of Inverness, on the ground of unhealthy competition.

After a long hearing, the bill was thrown out. The findings of the Parliamentary committee were, however, somewhat incongruous. While admitting that the Highland had not given sufficient facilities for the through traffic, and that unnecessary delays had occurred, it did not consider that the position warranted the granting of running powers, as it held the opinion that an amicable settlement under the existing régime was all that was needed. The committee expressed the hope that the two companies would be able to settle their differences to the improvement of the service.

In the midst of these troublous times, the Highland Railway suffered the loss of Andrew Dougall, the general manager, who retired at the close of the year 1896. A native of Perthshire, Dougall had gained railway experience, as a young man, in the south of Scotland, before entering the service of the Inverness & Nairn Railway in 1854. On the completion of that undertaking in the following year, he was appointed general manager, and shortly afterwards assumed the dual office of general manager and secretary. As the years passed by, his duties were increased to embrace the secretaryship of the nominally independent lines, subsequently amalgamated with the Highland Railway. He had seen the system grow, and none knew better than he its particular needs or the peculiar difficulties under which it laboured.

The acrimonious joint board meetings of the early days were

for him a vivid memory, and 35 years later his energies were
devoted to maintaining the Highland capital as a close preserve
of the company he served. In Andrew Dougall, William Moffatt
found a worthy adversary, who successfully resisted all attacks,
although it was left to his successor, Charles Steel, to lead the
Highland to victory in the last battle for Inverness.

The findings of the Parliamentary committee of 1895 gave
satisfaction to neither side. The Great North alleged that the
through coaches between Inverness and Aberdeen were mono-
polized, on the Highland Railway, by local passengers, with
the result that through passengers frequently had to change at
Elgin or Keith. After a great deal of argument, it was allowed
to send an attendant with the through trains, to ensure that
only passengers for its line used the through coaches.

The Great North also stressed the point that the population
on the Craigellachie line was greater than that on the Highland
Railway's route, via Mulben, and that most of the through
trains should take this route. The Highland, for its part, took
the view that its route was the shorter, and as the primary
function of the through trains was to serve passengers travelling
between Inverness and Aberdeen, they should go by the most
direct route.

Complaints were received that the Great North was un-
necessarily diverting traffic over its line by refusing to stop the
best trains at Keith. In defence of this action, it was argued
that the junction station at Keith was not so centrally situated
as Keith Town, on the Craigellachie line. For whatever reason
the stop at Keith was omitted, it had the effect of causing
through traffic to be handed over at Elgin in many cases.

Matters were in this unsatisfactory state in 1897, when the
Great North came forward with a second bill for running
powers between Elgin and Inverness. On this occasion it
sought to overcome the obstacle of single-line working by
offering to bear the expense of doubling the Highland Railway
from Elgin to Dalcross, from which point it was already double
into Inverness. The hearing of the bill occupied several days.
At first it appeared that the promoters were making a good

impression but, in the end, the tide turned in favour of the Highland, and the measure was rejected.

After the defeat in 1897, the Great North made no further attempts to enter Inverness. A basis of agreement was reached with regard to the through trains, and Elgin became the chief point of exchange. For some years engines were changed at the junction station, but in 1908 it was agreed that certain trains should be worked throughout by the engine of one company. This arrangement remained in force until shortly after the outbreak of the First World War.

UNION PROPOSED

To such an extent did relations between the two companies improve that towards the end of 1904 the question of amalgamation was mooted. The idea took definite shape in the course of the following year, and it was finally proposed that the union should become effective on January 1st, 1907. Opposition to the scheme came from certain Scottish and English railways, and from the town of Inverness, where it was feared, not without good reason, that the fusion would result in the removal of the cramped locomotive and carriage shops to the new works of the Great North of Scotland Railway at Inverurie. The step was rendered the more likely by the attitude of the town council over the question of petty customs.

By ancient right, the Burgh of Inverness levied petty customs dues on cattle and goods brought into the town. By the beginning of the present century these payments had reached an estimated total of £1,800 per annum, of which sum the Highland Railway paid a considerable proportion. The total abolition of the dues had been contemplated for some time, but definite action towards this end had been delayed. Prior to 1904, the Highland Railway had allowed the council's officers access to its books to determine the amounts due from traders and others, but in that year the Company refused to continue these facilities, and stated that henceforth it intended to give information only in respect of goods for which the railway itself was liable to pay. At the first half-yearly meeting in 1904 it was stated that unless the dues were soon abolished, it would be necessary to remove the locomotive works and the coal depot in order to escape the imposition.

At that time the council did not take this threat seriously and, pending a definite legal settlement, barriers were erected in the street at the Company's boundary to prevent goods from leaving the railway premises before the dues had been paid. Early in 1905 the Court of Session gave judgement in favour of the railway, but the council decided to carry the matter further, and the dispute was still unsettled when the announcement of the proposed amalgamation was made. Faced with the prospect of a serious loss of trade in the town, the council, on October 2nd, unanimously decided to oppose the bill, while seeking a conciliation with the railway Company. One speaker even went so far as to say that 'although regrettable things had been done by the town council in connexion with petty customs, still the town had always had the best interests of the Highland Railway at heart'. One month later it was decided to make application for the postponement of the council's action against the railway Company in respect of the latter assisting to collect the dues. This decision was followed by action to secure the total abolition of the dues.

Meantime, the amalgamation scheme had gone ahead, and the question was put to a vote of the Highland shareholders on March 7th, 1906. Although the result showed a majority in favour of the bill, not only was there a substantial opposition, but large numbers did not record a vote. In the report issued by the board it was stated that

> In consequence of the substantial opposition among the Shareholders towards the Bill for amalgamation with the Great North of Scotland Railway, and of the indifference shown by a large number of the Shareholders, who did not vote at all, and considering that in a matter of such importance they ought not to proceed except with the approval of

such a majority as would amount practically to unanimity, they had resolved, after consultation with the representatives of the Great North of Scotland Railway, to withdraw the Bill.

Thus did a modicum of opposition, strengthened by an inordinate amount of apathy, rob northern Scotland of the benefits of amalgamating two relatively small railways into a combined system with a route mileage of slightly less than 850. The scheme was never revived, and the two companies which had been so long estranged, only to come within an ace of fusion, were finally sundered by the terms of the Railways Act of 1921.

CHAPTER NINE

GROWTH OF TRAIN SERVICES

FIRST PERIOD: 1855–63

THE DEVELOPMENT of the train services of the Highland Railway falls naturally into three periods. The first represents the railway as a more or less local concern, dependent for its outlet to the south on the circuitous route of the Great North of Scotland Railway via Aberdeen; the second is ushered in by the opening of the direct line from Forres to Perth; and the final stage is reached in 1898, when the shortened route to Inverness, via Carr Bridge, was completed.

In November 1855 a service of five trains in each direction was provided on the Inverness & Nairn Railway. Most of the trains called at all stations, and required 45 to 50 m. for the journey of 15 miles. One, however, was faster, and carried the mails. It called at Fort George only, and completed its journey in 35 m.

The connexion beyond Nairn was by coach to Huntly, whence the Great North of Scotland Railway continued to Aberdeen. Three trains in each direction had Aberdeen connexions. The fastest time was made by the down mail, which left Aberdeen at 3 PM and reached Inverness at 11.31 PM. The up mail was 17 m. slower, and left Inverness at the inconvenient time of 12.40 AM. This hour of departure was necessary in order to connect with the train leaving Aberdeen for the south at 9.45 AM. The journey by the other trains took about ten hours.

When the Great North was extended to Keith, and the coach journey became shorter, the times of the Inverness & Nairn Company's trains were slightly altered. The up mail began to leave at 1.30 AM, and reached Aberdeen at 9.42 AM, a gain of an

hour. In the opposite direction the arrival time was 10.59 PM,
a gain of 30 m. In June 1857 only two connexions in each
direction were provided, but when the railway was opened to
Keith, in 1858, four trains were provided in each direction.
With the exception of the mails, which omitted a few stops,
trains called at all stations. The up mail left Inverness at
3.50 AM, and reached Aberdeen in less than six hours. The
corresponding down train was slower.

By March 1859 the train service south of Aberdeen had
been speeded up, and the Great North was able to start its
down mail train at 1.17 PM, Keith being reached at 3.57 PM.
The connexion for Inverness left at 4.12 PM, and calling at all
stations reached its destination at 7.2 PM. The up mail left at
6.40 AM, and reached Keith at 9 AM, and Aberdeen at 11.55 AM.
The other services had also improved slightly.

Four trains were run in each direction, calling at all stations,
when the northern main line was opened to Dingwall in 1862,
and extended to Invergordon in the following year. The average time was about 1 h. 40 m. for the journey of 31 miles.
Three trains in each direction had connexions to or from the
Great North of Scotland Railway. Sunday services were
limited to the main-line mail trains, which ran to their weekday
schedules.

On the ill-fated Findhorn branch four trains were run in
each direction until 1864. For a short time during that year the
number was increased to five, but the additional service was
soon withdrawn. The Burghead branch had three trains in
each direction.

SECOND PERIOD: 1863–98
(SOUTHERN MAIN LINE)

With the opening of the line from Forres to Perth, the train
services underwent a complete change. Connexions were given
to the same up and down mail trains as before, but the shorter
route permitted of greatly reduced overall times. For some
time there were two through trains in each direction between

Perth and Inverness. The down mail train left Perth at 9.30 AM, in connexion with the train leaving London (Euston) at 8.40 PM on the previous evening. Inverness was reached at 4.20 PM after calls at all stations. The second train left at 1 PM, and omitting some half-dozen stops reached Inverness at 7 PM.

The up mail left Inverness at 8 AM, and calling at all stations reached Perth at 3.30 PM. Passengers arrived in London at 4.37 the next morning. The second up train left at 1.5 PM and reached Perth at 7. Like the midday down train, it passed about half a dozen stations.

In addition to the trains performing the complete journey, an early-morning train ran from Kingussie to Inverness, and a corresponding return train in the evening. There were also two trains in each direction between Perth and Blair Atholl. Most of these local trains were mixed and very slow.

By March 1865 the down mail had been speeded up by the omission of several stops, and reached Inverness at 2.45 PM. The midday down train now called at all stations, and leaving Perth at 12.50 PM reached Inverness at 7.20 PM. In the opposite direction the up mail left at 10.18 AM and reached Perth at 3.33 PM. The second train was now slow, and required 6 h. 20 m. to reach Perth.

In the following year, two new down trains were put on. The first, running in connexion with the 10 AM from Euston, left Perth at 1 AM as a mixed passenger and goods train. Inverness was reached at 9 AM after stops at nearly all stations. The second train, with no London connexion, left Perth at 4.10 PM, and omitting about six stops reached Inverness at 10.10 PM. In the up direction a new train left Inverness at 6.30 AM and reached Perth at 1 PM after calling at all stations.

These services continued for some years with only a few detail alterations, but the 6.30 AM up and 4.10 PM down trains ran during the summer only. The midday down train also began to run about an hour earlier. In 1873 an extra down train was put on, leaving Perth at 10.10 AM, and reaching Inverness at 5.55 PM, after many stops. The service lasted five years, and ran during the early part of August only.

It was not until 1872 that a night train was run in the up direction. For some years it left Inverness at 7.30 PM, and reached Perth at 5.5 AM, but in 1878 it was altered to start at 10 PM and arrive at Perth at 7 AM. A sleeping-car was now run between Inverness and Perth. A connecting train reached London at 9.40 PM.

By 1881 the night train from London had been speeded up, and the down mail left Perth at 9 AM, reaching Inverness at 1.30 PM, an improvement of 45 m. on the Highland Railway. The bulk of this saving was achieved by the train running non-stop from Perth to Blair Atholl in 55 m. at 38 mph. The 9.30 now became a slow train, running as far as Blair Atholl only, but a few years later it began to run right through to Inverness in the summer only. The midday up train had also been improved. It now left at 1.30 PM, but reached Perth at 7 PM as before. Two years later the early-morning up and the afternoon down trains began to run throughout the year.

In July 1883 there were four trains in each direction between Perth and Inverness. Most of them still stopped many times, and required 5¾ to 7 h. for the journey of 144 miles. The best time was made by the down mail which covered the distance in 4½ h. with 11 intermediate stops. The best up train (the 10.10 AM from Inverness) required 5 h. 23 m., but this was 8 m. slower than in 1880. The 1.30 PM from Inverness took 5½ hours.

Two years later there was a big change for the better. Previously, with the exception of the 9 AM from Perth which ran non-stop to Blair Atholl, and the 1.30 PM up train which called only at Dunkeld between Blair Atholl and Perth, no fast trains of any sort had been run. In that year, however, the Highland Railway began to run the connexions to the London mail trains to much faster schedules. Improvements had been made south of Perth, and the Highland was able to start its train at 7.50 AM. Inverness was reached at 11.50 AM.* In the

---

*A four-hour schedule for the mail trains in each direction had been proposed by the Post Office in 1863, but the idea was abandoned on the grounds of expense.

Miles from Perth	STATIONS.	1	2 MIX. 1 & Pl.	3 MIXD. 1,2,Pl.	4 MIXD. 1,2,Pl.	5 MIXD 1 & Pl.	6 LIMD. MAIL 1,2,Pl.	7	8 PASS. 1,2,Pl.	9 PASS. 1,2,Pl.	10 EXC'N 1 & 3	11 PASS. 1,2,Pl.	12 MIXD. 1,2,Pl.	SUNDY MAIL 1,2,Pl.
	London, L. & N.W. dep			10 0A						10 0r			5 15A	8 50P
	Do. G.N. "			11 0	10 0		6 0r		8 50P	9 0			5 15	8 30
	Do. Midland "			10,35 10 35			8 0		8 30 8 25	9 15				8 25
	Glasgow, Buchanan St. "			9 25P			3 5A		7 10A 6 10	9 0A 8 30		2 0r 1 30	4 85p 3 55	9 20A 6 10
	Edinbro, Shrl. "			7 20 6 40			5 8		6 30 7 40	15	2 50P	1 30 3 30	6 0 6 40	
	Do. via Fife. "													
	Dundee. "													
				A.M.	A.M.		A.M.		A.M.	A.M.	P.M.	P.M.	P.M.	A.M.
41	Perth ....depart			12 40	6 10		7 50		9 30	11 50	3 30	4 30	7 25	8 50
7½	Luncarty .... "				6 20								7 35	
10½	Stanley .... "			1 0	6 35				9 45	12 10v	3 45	4 47	7 45	9 2
15½	Murthly .... "			1 12	7 0				9 51	12 23	3 55	4 55	7 55	9 8
20½	Dunkeld .... "			1 27	7 20				10 4	12 35	4 5	5 10	8 10	9 15
21¾	Dalguise .... "				7 35					12 46	Stop	5 22	8 22	
23¾	Guay .... "				7 42					12 61		5 26	8 30	
	Rallinluig .... "			1 50	7 50				10 22	1		5 32	8 40	9 34
32¾	Aberfeldy ....{depart arrive			2 5	9 0 8 5				9 45 10 55 10 33	12 20 1 35 1 16		6 10 5 43 5 52	9 15 8 55 9 5	9 42
28½	Pitlochry .... "				8 15					1 26		5 58	9	
32½	Killiecrankie .... "				8 15					1 26		5 52	9 5	
35¾	Blair-Athole .... "			2 25	8 25		8 45		10 47	1 36		6 5	9 15	9 55
40	Struan .... "				Stop				10 56	1 50		6 14	Stop	10 8
51½	Dalnaspidal .... "			3 15						2 20				
58½	Dalwhinnie .... "			3 35					11 39	2 30		6 53		11 10
68½	Newtonmore.... "						A.M.			2 50				
71¾	Kingussie ...... "			4 10			9 50		12 6r	3 1		7 23		11 10
77½	Kincraig .... "									3 15		7 33		
83½	Aviemore .... "			4 40			8 40		12 23	3 27		7 45		11 31
88½	Boat of Garten . "			4 55			8 58		12 38	3 37		7 55		11 40
92½	Broomhill .... "						9 10			3 44				
96	Grantown .... "			5 15			10 25		12 53	3 52		8 10		11 55
104½	Dava .... "						9 45			4 9				
110½	Dunphail .... "			6 0			10 15		1 26	4 27		8 40		12 23
	Forres. ......arrive			6 30			10 35	11 0	4A	4 50		9 0		12 35
					Pass. 1,2,Pl.			Mixed 1 & Pl		Pass. 1,2,Pl.			Pass. 1,2,Pl.	
119½	Forres & Keith Trains, see p 8 depart			6 40A	8 50A		11 5A	11 25	1 50v	4 55		5 5		12 0
123½	Brodie. "			6 48	8 57			11 35				9 13		
128½	Dalric "			7 4	9 11		11 20	11 49	2 5	5 20		9 27		12 57
134½	Fort-George.... "			7 24	9 23			12 1r	2 21	5 33		9 40		
137½	Dalcross. "			7 33	9 29			12 7		5 41		9 44		
140½	Culloden. "			7 45	9 36			12 15		5 51		9 54		
146	Inverness. ....arrive			8 0	9 45		11 50	12 25	2 45	6 5		10 5		1 30
				Mixd. 1,2,pl.	Pass. 1,2,Pl.		Mail 1,2,Pl.		Pass. 1,2,Pl.		unx10pl	Mixd. 1,2,Pl.		Pass. 1,2,Pl.
144	Inverness .....depart			5 30A	9 Pl.		12 10r		3 15v	4 5r	7 25v			1 45v
145½	Clachnaharry .. "			5 35	9 5				3 19	4 10	7 30			1 48
147½	Bunchrew .... "			5 45	9 11				3 25	4 19	7 35			1 52
149½	Lentran .... "			5 55	9 18				3 31	4 29	7 42			1 58
151½	Clunes .... "				9 25				3 37	4 37	7 49			2 3
154	Beauly .... "			6 15	9 35		12 29		3 45	4 50	8 0			2 9
157	Muir of Ord...... "			6 30	9 46				3 55	5 3	8 9			2 17
160½	Conon .... "			6 45	9 57		P		4 12	5 14	8 19			
162½	Dingwall .... "			7 7	10 9		12 47		4 12	5 45	8 28			2 35
166½	Fowlis .... "				10 21				4 23	6 0	8 38			
169	Novar. .... "			7 30	10 28		1 3		4 33	6 13	8 45			2 49
172½	Alness .... "			7 55	10 37		1 9		4 43	6 20	8 55			2 56
175½	Invergordon.... "			8 7	10 47		1 15		4 46	6 40	9 2			3 3
178½	Delny .... "			8 20	10 56				4 54	6 52	9 13			
180½	Kildary .... "			8 28	11 1		1 29		4 58	7 0	9 20			3 18
183½	Nigg .... "			8 37	11 7				5 4	7 10	9 25			
184½	Fearn. .... "			8 55	11 12		1 33r		5 10	7 20	9 31			3 28
							1 44			7 33	9 45			
188½	Tain .... {arr. dep.			9 5 9 15	11 20 11 22		1 46 1 56		5 20 5 35	Stop	Stop			3 36 3 46
193½	Edderton .... "			9 40	11 37				5 45					
197½	Bonar-Bridge.. {arr. dep.			10 0 10 10	11 58 12 8r		2 18		5 55 6 5					
201½	Culrain Platform "			10 10	12 13									4
204½	Invershin .... "			10 25			2 20		6 15					4 16
205½	Lairg .... "	Pass.		10 55	12 32		2 30		6 22					4 29
210½	Rogart .... "	1 & Pl.		11 26	12 59		3 8		6 55					4 44
223½	The Mound...... "	9 0		11 40	1 9		3 14		7 2					4 55
226½	Golspie .... "	9 15		11,55	1 18		3 24		7 13					5 14
230	Dunrobin (Priv	9 4												
232½	Brora .... "	9 25		12 20P	1 35		3 37		7 23					5	
239½	Loth .... "	9 28		12 37	1 50				7 40					5
245½	Helmsdale...... "	9 40		12 55	2 10		4 1		7 55					5 51
254½	Kildonan .... "	10 4		Stop	2 35				stop					6
	Borrobol Plat... "						4							1
262	Kinbrace .... "	10 19			2 55		4							6
269½	Forsinard .... "	10 34			3 15		4 49							6 39
277½	Altnabreac .... "	10 51			3 40									
283½	Scotscaler .... "	11 10			4 0		5							7
289½	Halkirk .... "	11 17			4 20		5							
291½	Georgemas Jun..arr	11 23			4 15		5 33							7 23
	Do. dep. for Thurso	11 28			4 20		5 40							
293½	Thurso .... dep						5 10							7 0
298	Thurso .... arr	11 45			4 40		6 0A							7 50
294	Georgemas Jun. dep				4 25		5 35							7 25
297½	Bower. .... "				4 33		5 42							7 39
300½	Watten. .... "				4 42									
303½	Bilbster. .... "				4 50									
305½	Wick. .... arr				6 10		6 0A							8 0

A page from the timetable of July 1885

up direction the 1.30 began to leave at 3 PM, and ran to a similar schedule. A year later, a new train running in advance of the express was put on. It left Inverness at noon, and reached Perth at 6.30 PM. Subsequently this schedule was cut by 40 m. The timetables of the two expresses were:

Down Train			*Up Train*		
Perth ...	...	7.50 AM	Inverness	...	3.0 PM
Blair Atholl	...	8.45 AM	Nairn ...	...	3.25 PM
Kingussie	...	9.50 AM	Forres ...	...	{ 3.40 PM
Grantown	...	10.25 AM			{ 3.45 PM
Forres ...	...	{ 11.0 AM	Grantown	...	4.23 PM
		{ 11.5 AM	Kingussie	...	5.5 PM
Nairn ...	...	11.20 AM	Blair Atholl	...	6.5 PM
Inverness	...	11.50 AM	Perth ...	...	7.0 PM

When the heavy gradients and the long stretches of single line are taken into consideration, this represents no poor performance. Although the winter loads were light, those taken by the down train during the summer were frequently colossal.

Foxwell in *Express Trains English and Foreign* comments thus on this train:

In July and August this 7.50 train is the unique railway phenomenon. Passenger carriages, saloons, horseboxes and vans, concentrated at Perth from all parts of England, and intermixed to make an irregular caravan. Engines are attached fore and aft, and the procession toils pluckily over the Grampians. Thus, on August 7th, 1888, the train sailed out of Perth composed as follows:

L.B. & S.C.R.—Horsebox	Midland Rly. —Horsebox
L.B. & S.C.R.—Horsebox	L. & N.W.R. —Horsebox
L.B. & S.C.R.—Carriage Van	N.B.R. —Luggage Van
L.B. & S.C.R.—Horsebox	N.B.R. —Horsebox
L. & N.W.R. —Horsebox	N.B.R. —Horsebox
N.E.R. —Horsebox	N.B.R. —Horsebox
L. & N.W.R. —Saloon	E.C.J.S. —Sleeping Car
L. & N.W.R. —Luggage Van	G.N.R. —Saloon
Midland Rly. —Saloon	W.C.J.S. —Composite
Midland Rly. —Luggage Van	Midland Rly. —Composite
Midland Rly. —Carriage Truck	L. & N.W.R. —Luggage Van

L. & N.W.R. —Horsebox
W.C.J.S.—Composite
L. & N.W. R.—Horsebox
L. & N.W. R.—Meat Van
Highland Rly.—P.O. Van
Highland Rly.—Luggage Van
Highland Rly.—Third-Class Passenger
Highland Rly.—First-Class Passenger

Highland Rly.—Second-Class Passenger
Highland Rly.—Third-Class Passenger
Highland Rly.—Luggage Van
Highland Rly.—Third-Class Passenger
Highland Rly.—First-Class Passenger
Highland Rly.—Third-Class Passenger
Highland Rly.—Guard's Van

Nine companies, 36 carriages, two engines in front, 1 put on behind at Blair Atholl. Left Perth 20 minutes late; left Kingussie 72 minutes late.*

With few possible exceptions the whole of the passenger stock was six-wheeled, and all the horseboxes and carriage trucks four-wheeled. Nevertheless it is an extraordinary load for any railway's best regular express, since the train was in no sense a special. Even if the train had been divided at Perth the second portion probably would have lost more time while waiting for the first train to clear the long stretches of single line and for up trains to pass.

By 1891 the down mail was leaving Perth at 7.5 AM. The schedule was still 4 h., but the train called additionally at Boat of Garten. The down night train had been considerably speeded up. It left Perth at 12.15 AM and reached Inverness at 6.30 AM, an improvement of 65 m. In the following year a further 20 m. were gained, when the arrival time became 6.10, and in 1895 there was a further improvement of 25 m. The 10 PM from Inverness was leaving at 10.30, and reaching Perth at 7.45 AM, but in 1893 the arrival time of 7 AM was restored.

With the growth of the tourist traffic a special express was run in advance of the down mail. In 1890 this train left Perth at 7.10 AM, and calling only at Blair Atholl and Forres, reached Inverness at 11.30. This was 20 m. slower than the mail. In the following year the departure time became 5.55 AM, and extra stops were put in. The journey now occupied 4¾ h., but by 1893 it had been reduced to 4½ h.

* The above is a verbatim extract. The final note should read: '*Ten* Companies, *thirty-seven* carriages . . .' Even this load was exceeded on at least one occasion by the afternoon down train, which reached Inverness (very late) with no less than 40 vehicles.

The summer services of 1896 showed a great advance. The 3 PM up train was now divided. The first portion ran to the original schedule, and reached Perth at 7 PM, but the second, which conveyed the through sleeping-cars for London, left at 4.30 PM and reached Perth at 8.40, with six regular and two conditional stops. The down tourist express had been altered to leave Perth at 5.30 AM and reach Inverness at 9.40. The up night train had also been improved, and ran from Inverness to Perth in 6¼ h.

The summer services for 1898 are the last that can be considered in this second period. In August the down sleeping-car express was run in two portions. The first, which ran until the 12th only, left Perth at 5 AM, and the second at 5.30. Both trains reached Inverness in 4 h. 10 m. The down mail now left Perth at 6.15 AM and arrived at Inverness at 10.15. The down midday train had been divided, the second portion leaving Perth at 12.10 PM as a slow train.

In the up direction the 10.10 AM from Inverness was relieved by a new train, leaving at 9.20, and reaching Perth at 3.15 PM. The London sleeping-car express now left at 4.55 PM, and retained its former schedule, but the midday train had been speeded by 25 m.

Until 1878 Sunday services were restricted to the mail trains in each direction, which observed their weekday times. In that year, however, the up night train began to run on Sundays; it had never run on Saturday–Sunday nights, nor did it ever do so. This extra service remained in operation until 1891. Subsequently, only the mail trains were run. In 1881 the down service was altered to leave Perth at 8.50 AM (instead of 9.30) and reach Inverness at 1.30 PM.

SECOND PERIOD: 1863–98
(NORTHERN MAIN LINE)

The railway was extended from Invergordon to Meikle Ferry on June 1st, 1864, and to Bonar Bridge on October 1st following. For some years there were four trains in each direction between Inverness and Tain, and three to Bonar Bridge, but when the railway was extended into Sutherland two trains only ran north of Tain. The speed of all these trains was little more than 20 mph, inclusive of stops at all stations.

At first, one train in each direction had a connexion to or from Perth, but from 1866 to 1868 three down trains and two up made connexion. Subsequently this number was reduced to two for stations north of Tain. Coach connexions to and from the north were given to the mail trains in each direction.

When the railway was completed to Wick in 1874 the services were altered. An early train left Inverness at 4 AM (subsequently 5 AM) for Helmsdale, calling at all stations. It had no connexion from the south or east. This was followed by a connexion with the night train from Perth, leaving at 9.15, and reaching Wick at 4.20 PM after stops at all stations. A year or so later this train was 40 m. slower, but by 1881 it was leaving Inverness at 9 AM and reaching Wick at 5 PM. A similar train in connexion with the down mail left Inverness at 3.10 PM and reached Wick at 10.35 PM.

In the up direction a train left Wick at 4.45 and reached Inverness at 12.15 PM, after calling at all stations. This train connected with the 12.40 for Perth. A second train left at 11.50 and reached Inverness at 7 PM, whence the journey could be continued south by the night train. A train also left Bonar Bridge at 7.6 AM, arriving in Inverness at 9.50 in time to connect with the 10.18 AM for Perth. There was also a train from Helmsdale at 9.44 AM, which ran as far as Dingwall.

In the following year the 4.45 from Wick was altered to leave at 1 AM, and reach Inverness at 9.50. North of Tain it was a mixed train. The second train now left at 11.30 AM, but still reached Inverness at 7 PM. There was now no connexion north of Tain to the 12.40 PM from Inverness. The morning train from Helmsdale to Dingwall had been made earlier, and there was a corresponding return train from Dingwall to Tain. By 1880 the up train was leaving Helmsdale at 6.10 AM and running through to Inverness in 5 h. 50 m., to connect with the midday service to the south. There were also some local trips between Thurso and Wick.

During the months July to October inclusive, in 1878 to 1885, a morning train conveying first-class and parliamentary third-class passengers only, was run on certain days of the week (originally Saturdays, but latterly Tuesdays and Fridays and finally on Fridays only) between Golspie and varying destinations north thereof. At the outset Forsinard was the terminus, then Thurso, Wick and finally back to Thurso again. It returned in the late afternoon, reaching Golspie about 7 PM. As the working timetables show, these trains were worked by the Duke of Sutherland's private engine which, along with the coaches, was kept at Brora at this time.

When the down mail was expedited in 1881 to reach Inverness at 1.30 PM the connexion for the north was altered to leave at 2 PM and run to a faster schedule, certain small stations being omitted. Wick was reached at 8 PM, a gain of 70 m. In the up direction the former 1 AM from Wick was altered to leave at 12.10 AM, and slowed by 40 m.

The speeding-up of the services on the southern main line in 1885 caused several alterations north of Inverness. The 9 AM remained, but the 2 PM was altered to leave at 12.10. It retained its six-hour schedule. Its place in the afternoon was taken by a slow train leaving Inverness at 3.15, and running as far as Helmsdale, where it arrived at 7.55 PM. This train connected in the summer only with the 9.30 AM from Perth. The 11.30 AM from Wick was made much earlier, leaving at 8 AM and reaching Inverness at 2.30 PM, to connect with the 3 PM for the south. This was the last up train from Wick, but a new train was put on, leaving Helmsdale at 2.20 PM and reaching Inverness at 7.20, whence the journey could be continued to Perth by the night train.

Further changes were made in 1892 when the early train from Inverness was altered to leave at 6.30 AM, thus affording a connexion to the night train from Perth, which arrived at 6.10. It was also extended through to Wick, where it was due at 1.25 PM. The 9 AM from Inverness now ran as far as Helmsdale only, by which time it was only 30 m. in advance of the mail, leaving Inverness at 11.25 AM. The mail passed the slower train, which followed on to Wick some 50 m. later, serving some of the smaller stations omitted by the preceding train. This arrangement was only in force for a year or two, after which the 9 AM from Inverness did not run beyond Tain. This left certain stations north of Helmsdale with only one down train per day.

In the up direction, the afternoon train from Helmsdale was altered to start from Wick at 2.45, Inverness being reached at 9.25 PM. This was a great improvement, as for some years the last through train had left Wick at the very early hour of 8 AM. These alterations resulted in the uneven service of three up trains and two down. In 1895 the 12.10 AM from Wick was suspended, but the early train from Helmsdale was retimed to leave at 5.20 AM, and reach Inverness at 9.45 AM, to make connexion with the 10.10 AM for the south.

In the following year the 5.20 from Helmsdale was started from Wick at 2.30 AM, but this only lasted for a short while. However, for many years a peculiar arrangement was in force which gave additional facilities north of Helmsdale. First-class passengers were permitted, on signing an 'indemnity form' (absolving the railway Company from all liability for injury) to leave Wick at 1 AM by the night goods train. At Helmsdale they could transfer to the early morning train for Inverness. A similar arrangement was in force for the afternoon train from Inverness.* During the summer of 1896 the 3.10 PM down train ran as far as Tain only, being followed at 5.15 by a connexion with the midday train from Perth. The new train ran non-stop from Inverness to Dingwall, and then called at all stations to Wick, which was reached at 11.20 PM. This fore-runner of the 'Further North Express' only lasted a short while, however, after which the 3.10 PM was once more ex-tended to Helmsdale.

In the remaining two years of the period the only important

---

*Passengers could also travel by goods train on certain other parts of the system.

change was the alteration of the down mail. When the connexion from Perth began to reach Inverness at 10.15 AM the
train for Wick was automatically made to start at 10.35, and
retaining its schedule of six hours reached Wick at 4.35 PM.
The gradual improvement of the morning mail trains from
Perth to Inverness had resulted in a retrograde step on the
northern main line, as the last departure from Inverness for
stations north of Helmsdale became progressively earlier.

The Sunday train services call for little comment. For some
years the connexions to the up and down mail trains ran to
their weekday schedules. When the line was opened to Wick,
the up Sunday train left the northern terminus at the inconvenient hour of 2.30 AM and arrived in Inverness at 9.50 AM.
This was over two hours faster than the 12.10 AM weekday
train, but on Sundays no goods wagons were attached. The
down train from Inverness ran to the same schedule on Sundays as on weekdays.

SECOND PERIOD: 1863–98 (OTHER SERVICES)

As soon as the direct line from Forres to Perth was opened, the
services on the Keith line became of secondary importance.
The majority of the trains called at all stations and required
about $2\frac{3}{4}$ h. for the journey of 55 miles. At Keith the Great
North of Scotland Railway provided connexions to about three
trains in each direction, and the overall time between Inverness
and Aberdeen varied from $5\frac{1}{4}$ h. (by the early morning up
mail) to $7\frac{3}{4}$ h. The average time for the 108 miles was slightly
less than 6 h. For a short time the mail trains ran on Sundays
and weekdays, but by 1865 they had been withdrawn between
Aberdeen and Keith, although the Highland Railway continued to provide one train in each direction between Keith
and Forres.

By February 1872 the services were slightly better. The
trains still called at nearly all stations, but the best time from
Aberdeen to Inverness had been reduced to $4\frac{1}{2}$ h. This train

started at 10.15 AM and ran semi-fast to Keith, where it arrived at 12.25 PM. The connexion on the Highland Railway left 10 m. later. On the other hand, the best train in the opposite direction still required 5½ h.

The sweeping changes that followed William Moffatt's appointment as general manager of the Great North began to be apparent in 1885. In November of that year the number of connexions had been increased to four in each direction. The 10.10 AM from Aberdeen ran to Keith in 96 m., and Inverness was reached at 1.30 PM. The remaining trains occupied 4½ to 5 h. on the journey. For some obscure reason the eastbound service was slower, the best train (4 PM from Inverness) requiring 5 h., but this included a wait of 45 m. at Keith, as against 4 m. in the opposite direction. This performance was very nearly equalled by two trains which took about 10 m. longer.

Prior to 1886, no attempt had been made to exchange traffic at Elgin, but following the completion of the railway from Keith to Elgin, via the coast, the Great North made certain alterations in services which gave passengers the option of changing at either station by one or two trains in each direction. A few years later at least one train was making connexion at Elgin only.

A new early-morning train was put on, leaving Aberdeen at 3.35 AM, and reaching Keith at 5.25. The Inverness connexion left 10 m. later and arrived at 7.55. Subsequently this schedule was slightly eased. The 10.10 AM ex-Aberdeen still reached Keith at 11.46 AM, but the Highland connexion did not leave until 12.10 PM (instead of 11.50 AM) and made several extra stops. It arrived in Inverness at 2.15 PM, a deceleration of 20 m.

These services continued for some years with only a few slight changes, save that the 10.10 AM from Aberdeen was altered to leave 40 m. earlier and run correspondingly earlier throughout. In 1894 a new train was put on, leaving Inverness at 8.45 AM and reaching Keith at 11.5, where it connected with an express reaching Aberdeen at 12.55 PM.

When, as a result of the race of 1895, the competing night trains from London began to reach Aberdeen at about 6.30 AM, the Great North put on a new train in connexion, leaving at 6.45 AM. For a short while the arrival time at Elgin was 9.15, but subsequently several stops were cut out and the train reached Elgin (via the coast) at 8.48. The Highland Railway had a slow train leaving Elgin for Inverness at 8.53 AM, but the connexion with the GNSR arrival at 8.48 was not guaranteed. To make certain of reaching Inverness at 10.15 AM, passengers from Aberdeen by the 6.45 AM had to travel in the back part of the train (detached at Huntly) and join the Highland train at Keith. This was a typical example of the lack of facilities in the days of the 'warfare', and one that led to many bitter complaints.

By May 1897 a great improvement had taken place. The Great North had inserted several stops in the schedule of the 6.45 AM from Aberdeen, which now reached Elgin at 9. The Highland ran a train in connexion at 9.10, which joined the morning mail from Perth at Forres. The journey from Elgin to Forres was performed non-stop in 17 m. Several other trains in each direction ran to corresponding schedules between Elgin and Forres, to the general betterment of the service. The best time from Aberdeen to Inverness became 3½ h., by two trains leaving at 6.45 AM and PM respectively. Two others were only 10 m. slower.

In the opposite direction the best time was 3 h. 5 m. by the 3 PM from Inverness, which ran via Keith. The 55 miles from Inverness to Keith were covered in 90 m., with stops at Nairn, Forres and Elgin. There was no corresponding return service. The best trains via Elgin required 3½ to 4 h. for the whole journey. These services remained in force until the end of the period under review.

When the railway was opened to Strome Ferry in 1870, two trains in each direction were provided. These called at all stations and required about 3 h. for the journey of 53 miles from Dingwall. The down trains ran in connexion with the night and morning mail trains from Perth. The up service was similarly arranged. The morning down and the afternoon up trains connected at Strome Ferry with the Hebridean steamers. These services continued for many years with only minor alterations.

For a considerable period the second down and the first up trains were suspended during the winter, but later on two trains in each direction were run throughout the year, and a third during the summer. By 1885 the morning mail train from Perth had been improved sufficiently to allow the steamer connexion to be provided by the second train from Dingwall. A few years later it became the practice to work certain trains through to and from Inverness, instead of attaching the coaches to main-line trains, or making passengers change at Dingwall.

The Skye line never enjoyed Sunday services. In all probability, lightness of traffic was the determining factor. On the other hand, the people of Wester Ross were evidently strict sabbatarians in the early days of the railway. Pendleton, in *Our Railways*, records a serious disturbance which occurred at Strome Ferry in 1883, when it was desired to run a Sunday fish special:

A remarkable scene was witnessed at Strome Ferry – on (Sunday) June 3rd, 1883. The people were determined at all hazards that others besides themselves should keep the Sabbath. The Railway Company proposed to send a load of fish by special train, so that the provender might be taken on by the limited mail (from Inverness). When the fishing boats came inshore to unload, the villagers mustered, armed with clubs and sticks. They menaced the crews, and prevented the landing of the fish. Not only the police, but the railway officials interfered; but the combined forces were overcome by the indignant coast-dwellers, who took possession of the pier and the station.

The crowd prayed and sang in the railway station and – actually remembered the Directors in their supplications – until midnight, when traffic was resumed. Ten of the men, found guilty of mobbing and rioting, were sent to prison for four months each. The riot was the subject of questions in the House of Commons, and Sir William Harcourt, then Home Secretary, replied that if the men had really expressed sincere regret he would consult with the judge with a view to securing a remission of the sentence. He did consult with his lordship; and on September 23rd the men were liberated from Calton Jail, Edinburgh.

The minor branches call for little notice. In the majority of cases, four or five trains were run in each direction, on weekdays only. They called at all stations, and speeds were low. Mixed trains were run on certain services. From October 1863 to May 1867 a morning and afternoon service was provided in each direction on the Inverness harbour branch; possibly they connected with coastal steamers at the harbour.

THIRD PERIOD: 1898–1922
(SOUTHERN MAIN LINE)

The opening of the direct line to Inverness, via Carr Bridge, caused big alterations in the train services. Most of the trains were diverted to the new line, and the journey time between Perth and Inverness was reduced by about one hour. Connexions for the older route were provided at Aviemore.

The morning mail still left Perth at 6.15 AM, and reached Aviemore at 8.30. Leaving at 8.35, it arrived in Inverness at 9.30. To cover the $34\frac{1}{2}$ miles of steeply-graded line at an average speed of 37.6 mph was a distinctly good performance. The special summer tourist express was similarly expedited. The down night train left Perth at 12.50 AM, and Aviemore at 3.55, reaching Inverness at 5.10 (subsequently 4.56). The 9.25 AM from Perth was continued during the winter, and reached Inverness at 1.30 PM. Later on, the arrival time became 1.50. The midday and afternoon trains called at all stations on the new line, but reached Inverness over an hour earlier than before.

In the up direction the early morning train left Inverness at 7.20 and reached Perth at 11.30. For the time being the 9.20 AM relief train was suspended north of Aviemore, but was later restored, in summer, to leave Inverness at 10.10, and run via Forres. The 10.10 AM from Inverness was altered to leave at 11.10, and run via the new line. It reached Perth at its old time of 3.33 PM. The 3.5 PM left at 3.50, and was booked to Aviemore in 60 m., where it took up its old schedule. In summer a relief train was run via Forres. For some time it followed the main express from Aviemore, but later ran in advance right through to Perth. The original midday relief train survived as a slow train leaving Inverness at 2 PM, and reaching Perth at 6.40, via Carr Bridge. In 1902, it was diverted via Forres, and considerably slowed. A year later it was curtailed to start from Grantown during the summer, and from Blair Atholl in the winter.

The summer sleeping-car express for London was altered to start at 5.45 PM, and reach Perth at 9.25, a gain of 30 m. This schedule was soon eased, and by 1904 the train was leaving Inverness at 5 and reaching Perth at 9.5. The night train for Perth continued to run via Forres, and the schedule was slightly eased.

In the summer of 1900 a new evening express was put on, leaving Perth at 8.15. It included through coaches leaving London (King's Cross and Euston) at 10 AM. Stops were made at Pitlochry, Blair Atholl and Kingussie, and the train reached Inverness at 11.30 PM. A corresponding up train, calling additionally at Aviemore, left Inverness at 8.50 AM, and reached Perth at noon, in time for the midday departures for London. The down service ran in the summer only, but the up train was continued throughout the year, and was expedited to reach Perth at 11.56 AM, thus becoming the fastest train on the line. It ran from Blair Atholl to Perth in 46 m., at a speed of 46 mph.

In the summer of 1902 the down train was diverted via Forres, and considerably slowed by the inclusion of several regular and conditional stops. It did not reach Inverness until

12.10 AM. In 1904 it was altered to leave Perth at 7.5 PM, and reach Inverness at 11.10. Good connexions were provided from Edinburgh, Glasgow and the North of England, but London passengers had to leave Euston at 5.15 AM. The train was withdrawn as usual during the following winter, and never reinstated. The primary reason for the failure of the northbound service to become a regular feature of the summer timetables appears to have been the refusal of the Highland Railway to maintain the connexion at Perth when the trains from the south were running late (by no means uncommon in those days).

For several years the services continued almost unaltered. The 8.50 AM from Inverness was slowed by 10 m., and made to start at 8.40. During the winter it called at all stations between Inverness and Aviemore, but the schedule for the 34½ miles remained 63 m. The up night train still ran via Forres, but was slightly accelerated. In the opposite direction, during the summer, the first part of the midday train from Perth was shown as running non-stop to Newtonmore, but a stop was usually made at Blair Atholl for water and banking assistance. This train reached Inverness via Forres. After 1911 the 9.25 AM from Perth ceased once more to run to Inverness during the winter, and terminated at Blair Atholl.

The provision of sleeping-cars from London to Inverness via the East Coast, West Coast and Midland routes did not prove an unmixed blessing to the Highland Railway. The cars were well patronized during the summer, but in the winter months the number of through passengers was small. The Highland Railway naturally objected to hauling this extra load over its mountainous road with but little prospect of an adequate return, and in 1903 suggested to the English companies that in subsequent winters each should run one car twice per week. This arrangement, together with interavailability of tickets, would have assured passengers of a through service every night in each direction.

The English companies agreed, but the Caledonian Railway objected, on the grounds that the North British Railway would haul four services between the Border and Perth, while it would work only the West Coast cars. It demanded to be allowed to haul one of the Midland services north of Carlisle. Over this trifling dispute negotiations broke down, and for the time being the sleeping-cars terminated at Perth, because the Highland Railway refused to take more than one car per night through to Inverness. Subsequently agreement was reached, and the Highland Railway's suggestion put into force. A few years later the Midland Railway withdrew its cars in the winter, and the service was provided to and from Euston and King's Cross on alternate nights.

The outbreak of war in August 1914 brought a vast amount of extra traffic to the Highland Railway. Until the end of 1916 the timetables did not show many important alterations or curtailments although the service provided during the summers of 1915 and 1916 was little better than that of a normal winter. The relief train to the regular midday service from Perth was continued throughout the winter of 1914, on Fridays only, but it did not survive after the following summer. On the other hand, the up night service from Inverness, which had run during the summer only after 1911, was continued throughout the year from 1915.

In the winter of 1915 the 9.30 AM stopping train from Perth to Blair Atholl continued to Inverness with only one advertised stop, at Kingussie. The time allowed from Blair Atholl to Kingussie was 58 m., and the final $46\frac{1}{2}$ miles to Inverness were scheduled in 99 m. This curious schedule remained in force until the end of 1916. The afternoon down train also worked to an unusual schedule. It ran non-stop to Dalnaspidal, but called at all stations thence to Inverness via Carr Bridge. This working was continued throughout the war period, although subsequently an additional stop, at Struan, was included.

In 1917 drastic alterations and curtailments were made. The night trains from London were considerably slowed, and the Highland Railway was unable to start the connexion from Perth until 7.15 AM. Inverness was reached at 11.10, a deceleration of 35 m. The through sleeping-cars were suspended. The

9.30 AM from Perth was withdrawn north of Blair Atholl, and the schedules of many other trains were eased. In the up direction the 8.40 AM from Inverness was suspended, and the 11.10 was altered to leave at 9.30 AM. It required 4½ h. to reach Perth, with many stops. The afternoon up train was also made slower.

The years following the war witnessed a gradual improvement. The summer sleeping-car expresses to and from London, and the relief trains, via Forres, to the mid-morning and afternoon departures from Inverness were restored in 1919. In the following year the 8.40 AM from Inverness was reinstated, but the arrival time in Perth (12.18 PM) did not allow of the journey to London being completed in the same day. This facility was restored in 1921, when the departure time from Inverness became 8.10 AM, and the train reached Perth at 11.28. In the winter of the following year the train reverted to its pre-war schedule, but it had been suspended during the winters of 1920 and 1921. The early-morning slow train from Inverness to Perth was not reinstated. In 1920 the up night train was altered to start at 11.20 PM, run via Carr Bridge, and reach Perth at 5.5 AM.

By the winter of 1922 the down morning mail was leaving Perth at 6.40 AM and reaching Inverness at 10.15. Certain other trains also showed slight improvement, but on the whole the schedules fell far short of their pre-war levels. The summer of that year saw the introduction of restaurant-car facilities. A Pullman car from the Caledonian Railway ran with the midday train from Perth as far as Aviemore. It returned south with the afternoon train from Inverness. In the following autumn a restaurant car from the Great North of Scotland Railway worked through to Inverness on the 8.5 AM train from Aberdeen, and returned with the midday service. Previously passengers had been obliged to rely on the station refreshment rooms, and many of the trains waited for some minutes at Kingussie and Bonar Bridge for that purpose.

Sunday services were still restricted to one mail train in each direction. The schedules remained almost unaltered, and

the trains travelled via Forres. From 1911 to 1914 a down
relief train was run during the summer only, leaving Perth
20 m. in advance of the mail, but there was no corresponding
up service. In 1916 the trains were diverted to the Carr Bridge
route, and ran non-stop between Aviemore and Inverness.
For the time being Nairn and Forres were served by connecting
trains from Inverness, but these facilities were soon withdrawn.

In 1920 the Postmaster-General decided to suspend the
Sunday deliveries of letters throughout the country. In consequence the Sunday train service between Perth and Inverness
was withdrawn. The connecting trains on the northern main
line shared a like fate, and at the grouping the passenger
services on the Highland Railway were restricted to weekdays
only.

THIRD PERIOD: 1898-1922
(NORTHERN MAIN LINE)

For several years after 1898 no radical changes were made in the
train services north of Inverness. The earlier arrivals from the
south enabled the connecting trains to leave correspondingly
earlier, but the schedules remained almost unaltered. The
connexion to the down night train now left Inverness at
5.40 AM and reached Wick at 12.25 PM. The down northern
mail left at 9.50 AM, but still required 6 h. for its journey of
161¼ miles. This was the last departure from Inverness for
stations north of Helmsdale. In the opposite direction the
early train started from Helmsdale at 6 AM, and the morning
departure from Wick was at 8.40 AM. In each case, however,
the journey times remained almost unaltered. The afternoon
train from Wick ran to its former timing, as its connexion for
the south still travelled via Forres. Until the outbreak of the
war these services suffered no more than minor alterations.
Most of the changes tended towards easier schedules.

In the summer of 1906 the 'Further North Express' was
put on. The train ran on Fridays only, leaving Inverness at

Further North !

Further North !

FORTNIGHTLY PASSES

FOR

Visiting the Northern Highlands

From 1st JUNE UNTIL 30th SEPTEMBER, VISITORS from SOUTH and EAST of PERTH, holding RETURN TICKETS to NEWTONMORE or ANY STATION NORTH THEREOF, can obtain

FORTNIGHTLY PASSES

AVAILABLE BETWEEN

NEWTONMORE, FORRES, FORT-GEORGE, INVERNESS, FORTROSE, STRATHPEFFER, KYLE OF LOCHALSH, DORNOCH, THURSO, WICK, LYBSTER, and Intermediate Stations, at the undernoted Rates:—

FIRST CLASS.	THIRD CLASS.
£3.	**£2.**

The Passes will be available by any Ordinary Train during the Fortnight without limit as to the number of Journeys, provided they are used for Pleasure Excursions only.

They will not be available for Business Purposes.

Forms of Requisition can be obtained at any Station within the above-named area, or at the Traffic Manager's Office, Inverness, on presentation of the Return Half of Ticket from South or East of Perth.

Twenty-Four Hours' Notice will be necessary when the Passes are required at Stations outside Inverness.

An offer in the winter timetable of 1908

4.30 PM, in connexion with the 11.50 AM from Perth, and ran to Dornoch. It ran nominally non-stop to The Mound in 2 h. 35 m., and reached its destination at 7.33 PM. This distinctly easy schedule included stops for water. There was no corresponding return service.

At the conclusion of the summer service the train was altered to leave Inverness on Fridays only at 2.20 PM (in connexion with the 9.25 AM from Perth) and extended to Wick, where it was due at 7.25 PM, after calling at Dingwall, Tain, Bonar Bridge, Golspie, Helmsdale, Forsinard and Georgemas. An up express, running on Thursdays only, left Wick at 10.35 AM and reached Inverness at 3.30 PM, with six intermediate stops. The down train ran to this schedule for one winter only. In the following summer the original departure time (4.30 PM) was restored. Extra stops at The Mound and Brora were put in, and Wick was reached at 9.20 PM. The up train remained unaltered. These expresses ran throughout the year until the autumn of 1912, when they were withdrawn for the winter. In 1908 the down train was accelerated to reach Wick at 9.5 PM. It ran non-stop from Inverness to Tain in 65 m. (40.6 mph). In the winter it reverted to its slower schedule. During 1913 and 1914 the northbound train ran on Wednesdays and Fridays, and in the opposite direction the service was provided on Thursdays and Saturdays. Both services were withdrawn on the outbreak of the war and neither was restored until after the Highland Railway had become part of the L M S R in 1923.

A few years after the opening of the branch to Strathpeffer, a through train was run to the spa, on Saturdays only, starting from Inverness at 3 PM, and making connexion with the 9.25 AM from Perth. The train returned in the evening at 8.15 PM. In each direction stops were made only at Beauly, Muir of Ord and Dingwall. The departure time and the schedule varied slightly from year to year, but the service remained in operation until 1914.

On June 1st, 1911, the Highland Railway opened its hotel at Strathpeffer. To encourage traffic a through service from the

south was provided on Tuesdays only. The new train started
from Aviemore at 2.30 PM, in connexion with the 11.50 AM
from Perth, which reached Inverness via Forres. It ran non-
stop to Dingwall in 90 m., and thence to Strathpeffer, where it
arrived at 4.15 PM. Throughout the history of the Highland
Railway this was the only regular train that ran past Inverness
without stopping.* There was no corresponding service in the
up direction. The 'Strathpeffer Express' ran during the summer
only. It was finally withdrawn in the autumn of 1915, on
account of the war, and never reinstated. During its last
summer it started from Perth at 11.45 AM and called only at
Kingussie before running non-stop from Aviemore to Dingwall in 85 m. The 11.50 AM from Perth had been suspended,
and passengers for Inverness had to use the slower train leaving
at midday.

In common with all other services the trains on the northern
main line were decelerated during the war period, although
their number was not seriously reduced. Slight improvements
were made shortly before the grouping, but in December 1922
the schedules had not regained their 1914 standard.

THIRD PERIOD: 1898–1922 (OTHER SERVICES)

The opening of the shortened route to Inverness did not
materially affect the Aberdeen services. Most of the trains
continued almost unaltered, but the 6.45 AM from Aberdeen
was altered to leave 45 m. earlier, and reach Elgin at 8.20. The
connecting train on the Highland Railway was due in Inverness at 9.35, in time for the departure of the northern mail at
9.50. In summer the train ran every day, but after 1902 the
service was provided on Mondays only during the winter,
and the connexion with the Highland Railway was made at
Keith. In the opposite direction the 3 PM from Inverness was

*If the 11.50 AM from Perth was seriously delayed, the 'Further.
North Express' was also started from Aviemore, but the train called at
Inverness to pick up passengers.

changed to leave at 3.55, because of the later arrival of the train from Wick. It was considerably slowed by the inclusion of several stops, and did not reach Aberdeen until 7.20 PM. Some years later it was still further decelerated and required 4 h. 5 m. for the journey.

The services continued on these lines until the outbreak of the 1914 war. Such alterations as were made tended for the most part towards somewhat easier timings. In 1917 the trains were slowed and drastically reduced in number. Slight improvements were made in the years following the war, but, as with most other services, the recovery was by no means complete when the grouping came into force.

No radical changes were made on the long cross-country line to Kyle of Lochalsh in the autumn of 1898. The timetable was, of course, adjusted to suit the altered services on the southern main line, but the schedules remained almost unaltered. In summer four trains were run in each direction. For a few years three services each way were run in winter, but the timetable soon became unbalanced by the cancellation of one westbound train.

A fast train appeared in the summer of 1901. It left Dingwall at 10.36 (in connexion with the 9.50 AM from Inverness) and called only at Garve, Achnasheen and Strathcarron. Kyle of Lochalsh was reached at 1 PM. The ordinary mail train followed from Dingwall at 11.10 AM and continued to call at all stations. The new train ran during the summer only, and was finally withdrawn in the autumn of 1903. At no time was there a corresponding eastbound service, although for several summers the early-morning train from Kyle of Lochalsh connecting with the steamer from Stornoway only called conditionally at certain stations. It reached Inverness in time to allow passengers to catch the day train to London.

With the exception of the branch from Keith to Portessie, where services were completely suspended, no section of the Highland Railway suffered more drastic wartime reductions of services than the line from Dingwall to Kyle of Lochalsh. Such was the volume of special traffic arriving by sea at Kyle, and proceeding east by rail, that the service was ultimately reduced to one daily passenger train in each direction. Soon after the armistice, it was found possible to provide extra facilities, and by 1922 the service consisted of three eastbound and two westbound trains throughout the year. A third train ran from Dingwall to Kyle of Lochalsh on Wednesdays and Saturdays during the summer.

CHAPTER TEN

PROBLEMS OF OPERATION

SINGLE LINE AND ITS DIFFICULTIES

IN ONE respect the Highland differed from most British railways: the greater proportion of it was single track. When the Company received its Act of Incorporation in 1865, out of a route mileage of 242 the only double-track section was the $6\frac{3}{4}$ miles from Inverness to Dalcross, widened on October 1st, 1864. For many years this amount remained unaltered, because none of the extensions of the system was provided with a double line. The $7\frac{1}{4}$ miles from Perth to Stanley were also double, but the Highland Railway only exercised running powers over this section.

So long as the railway extended only from Inverness to Keith, serious delays do not appear to have been common, but as soon as the line from Forres to Perth was opened, the Company began to experience difficulty in getting the trains through to time, and great inconvenience to passengers often resulted. As an instance of this, the following extract from a letter, written from Perth in September 1863 a few days after the line had been opened, is illuminating:

Here we are safely landed, but by no means without adventure. While the Directors of the new line were complimenting each other, I wish they could have heard the other side of the question – the passengers' point of view of the new management. There was nothing but abuse of them on all sides, and regret that they should have opened the line before they could manage it properly and comfortably. Delay after delay occurred – want of water – waiting until this or that train should have passed – or dawdling from no visible cause whatever, until we were six hours too long on the road. The last train had left Perth for the south when we were only dragging through Dunkeld.

But the worst of it was that Perth was not equal to such an enormous influx of strangers, and we were all flying hither and thither in quest of beds of any sort. In our case the labour was in vain. We tried The British, The George, The Salutation, The Commercial, The Temperance, etc, besides lodging and private houses, but all were full. At last, thoroughly tired out, we came back to the station, and made up what sleeping places we could on the sofas and chairs in the Waiting Room. There were several other persons, with children, reduced to the same extremity, so you may be sure that there was but little quiet for rest and sleep. Morning, however, came at last. In the midst of our troubles, we were amused with a jolly Englishman in the train, who was making fun of the whole affair. He had left Inverness the day before, and had only got to Dalwhinnie at two o'clock in the morning. He betook himself, vexed and fatigued, to the hotel, and at four o'clock in the afternoon the train was still there. Here he was, getting into Perth on the second night by our train, and chaffing the guards with speeches such as: 'Extraordinary dispatch, Inverness to Perth in two days! Great cheapness, only two hotel bills besides the train fare!'

In fairness, it must be admitted that the unfinished state of the line and the steep gradients were largely responsible for this exceptional delay, although the long stretches of single line evidently played their part.

Punctuality on the Highland Railway was always adversely affected by two important factors: the long and steep gradients over the mountains, and the possibility of the connecting trains from the south reaching Perth much behind their scheduled times. As traffic developed, and trains increased in weight and frequency, serious delays became the rule. At periods of high

(1) Highland Railway, second-class single (colour: blue); (2) Duke of Sutherland's Railway, third-class return half (colour: green); (3) Highland Railway, third-class parliamentary, Culrain to Invershin, fare ½d (colour: green); (4) Inverness & Perth Junction Railway, first-class return half (colour: white); (5) Inverness & Aberdeen Junction Railway, third-class return (colour: green); (6) Highland Railway, first-class single (colour: white); (7) Highland Railway, third-class single (colour: green)

Top: Kyle of Lochalsh in the early 1900s. *Centre:* Forres from the west, showing Highland signals. *Bottom:* Keith station looking west

Top: Georgemas looking towards Wick. *Centre:* Blair Atholl about 1905. *Bottom:* Dingwall, looking south in the early 1900s

Top: Inverness train at Tain, with class '5' 4-6-o, in September 1959.
Centre: Strome Ferry in 1935. *Bottom:* New station at Lochluichart
opened in 1954

Top: Passenger-operated signals to stop train at Glencarron Platform.
Centre: Scottish Region type of nameboard at Strathcarron. *Bottom:*
The opening ceremony of the Duke of Sutherland's Railway, November 1st, 1870

Top: Dunrobin station, looking south, in LMSR days. *Centre:* Spey Viaduct, Orton, as rebuilt in 1906. *Bottom:* Viaduct over Tay at Dalguise

Top: Viaduct in the Pass of Killiecrankie. *Centre:* Bridge over the Garry and the road at Struan. *Bottom:* Bridge over the river at Conon, with Telford's road bridge in the background

Top: Train snowed up at Ardullie (Dingwall), December 1906.
Centre: Snow-plough at Achterneed, December 1906. *Bottom:*
Barclay 2-2-2 No 31, 'Princess', built in 1863

Top: No 7, built as a 2-4-0 in 1858 and converted to a 4-4-0 for the Skye line. *Centre:* No 65, 'Nairnshire', built in 1874, one of the first Jones 4-4-0s. *Bottom:* The first 'Skye Bogie', No 70, built in 1882

Top: 'Jones Goods' 4-6-0 No 105 at Inverness, 1898. *Centre:* The first 'Small Ben' 4-4-0, No 1, 'Ben-y-Gloe', built in 1898. *Bottom:* 'Castle' class 4-6-0 No 143, 'Gordon Castle', built in 1900

Top: No 68, one of Drummond's 0-6-4 tanks, built in 1909. *Centre:*
Smith's 4-6-0 No 70, 'River Ness', as delivered to the Highland
Railway in 1915. *Bottom:* No 73, 'Snaigow', one of Cumming's
4-4-0s, built in 1917

Top: One of the last locomotives built for the Highland Railway, 4-6-0 No 55, 'Clan MacKinnon', built in 1919. *Centre:* First-class coach No 36 at Aberfeldy, 1912. *Bottom:* Sleeping-car for Glasgow-Inverness service, built in 1907

Top: North side of Inverness station about 1906, after arrival of night train from London. *Centre:* Slochd Summit board, 1928. *Bottom:* Construction train at Duirinish in 1897

Top: Class '5' 4-6-0 entering Achterneed with an Inverness train in 1947. *Centre:* Train from Kyle of Lochalsh, headed by 'Loch' class 4-4-0 at Achterneed in the 1930s. *Bottom:* Third-class coach built about 1875

Top: 2-4-0 'Invergordon' on train at Thurso station about 1902.
Bottom: View at Kildonan station, August 1947

Top: Down train delivering tablet to signalman at Clachnaharry
Cabin, 1936. *Bottom:* Slochd North signal box, 1936

pressure, much time was lost at stations waiting for other trains to pass, and chaos ensued. Towards the end of the century, with the approaching completion of the direct line from Aviemore to Inverness, the problem was taken seriously in hand. On the new line, the 11 miles from Inverness to Daviot, covering the major portion of the formidable bank of 1 in 60, which begins almost as soon as the terminus is left, were constructed as a double road.

Meanwhile, steps had been taken to improve arrangements for single-line working. Until the early 1890s, the old-fashioned system of telegraphing passing orders for trains along the line had been in vogue, but the whole of the main lines and the more important branches were subsequently equipped with electric or tablet instruments. At a later date, automatic tablet exchange apparatus was introduced on the main lines, and many of the crossing loops were re-aligned to give the straighter road to the direction in which the faster running might be expected.

In 1897 parliamentary powers were obtained for doubling the line throughout between Stanley and Aviemore, including abolition of the 310-yard Murthly Tunnel, but only the portion over the Grampians was widened. The opening dates appear in Appendix V. Likewise, an ambitious scheme to double the line between Aviemore and Inverness was not proceeded with, but some relief was afforded by provision of extra crossing places between stations and a crossing loop at certain additional roadside stations; locations and opening dates are shown in Appendix II.

A further section of widening was put in hand a few years later, in much easier country immediately north of Inverness. The first 1¼ miles from Rose Street to Clachnaharry, were not included, because the doubling of this length would have necessitated widening of the bridges over the River Ness and the Caledonian Canal. Beyond Clachnaharry station, however, a double line was provided as far as Clunes, a distance of six miles. When completed in 1914, the double-line mileage on the Highland Railway was:

Section			Opening Date	Miles
Inverness to Dalcross	...	...	1864	6¼
Inverness to Daviot	...	...	1898	11
Blair Atholl to Dalwhinnie	...	1900–1909	23¼
Clachnaharry to Clunes ...	...	1913–1914	6
Total ...	...	...		47

Similar provision was made north of Clunes, reducing the single-line sections on the northern main line to about 5 miles, but the loop at The Mound could only be used for goods trains, or for one passenger and one goods train, as the station had only one platform on the main line; the side platform served the Dornoch branch.

For about 3 miles north of Boat of Garten, the main line of the Highland Railway paralleled the Great North of Scotland's Strathspey branch. This section was worked as two single lines, and the only physical connexion was immediately south of the station. The arrangement was adopted to save provision of a signal box at the point of divergence.

The track layout at Stanley

Another curious layout was at Stanley. Down trains for the Highland Railway were accommodated at an extension of the down platform, clear of the line to Aberdeen, while up trains used the outer face of the same platform, joining the Caledonian Railway south of the station. This arrangement enabled a Highland up train to clear the single line, and yet wait before proceeding towards Perth. In the same way, a Highland down train could stand at the platform until an up train had arrived, leaving both Caledonian roads clear.

THE HIGHLAND RAILWAY IN WARTIME

Immediately after the outbreak of war in 1914 the north of Scotland became of extreme strategical importance. The Fleet was already at Scapa Flow, in the Orkneys, and a permanent Naval base was established there. The nearest point of embarkation on the mainland was Scrabster Harbour, situated 2 miles from Thurso.

Farther south, at Invergordon, on the Cromarty Firth, a huge repair base for ships of war was established. The works included a new pier (carrying railway sidings, water mains, and oil-pipe lines), well-equipped engineering shops, stores and housing accommodation for about 4,000 workers. Situated 31 miles from Inverness, on the northern main line of the Highland Railway, Invergordon in pre-war days was little more than a village. It began to assume importance when the Admiralty adopted the Cromarty Firth as a practice base, and an oil-fuel depot was established there. The number of tanks was greatly increased in the early days of the war. Three large military camps, accommodating some 7,000 men, were also established in the vicinity. While these new works were in progress, every siding north of Perth was choked with wagons consigned to Invergordon which the main line of the Highland Railway was unable to accommodate.

The building of the defence works at Scapa Flow and the entrance to the Cromarty Firth brought a huge timber traffic to the Highland Railway. Whole trainloads of heavy baulks were sent to Scapa for this purpose. Simultaneously came an urgent and ever-increasing demand for pit-timber to be sent southwards, and large areas in the north of Scotland were completely denuded of trees. This work was performed largely by the Canadian Forestry Battalion, but, in certain cases,

German prisoners were employed. By 1918 this class of traffic had increased to ten times its normal amount.

Prior to the war, coal for the north of Scotland was carried almost exclusively by coaling steamers. The bulk of this traffic was subsequently transferred to the railway, and there were occasions when the sidings of nearly all the stations between Inverness and Wick were blocked with coal wagons which could not be moved because of the congested state of the lines. The Highland Railway, on whose system there were no coalfields, had to obtain from collieries south of Perth the greatly-increased quantities of locomotive coal required for working the heavy additional traffic. Fortunately the Company was not called upon to handle the huge supplies of Admiralty coal required at Scapa. These were taken by rail to Grangemouth Docks, on the Firth of Forth, and shipped thence by sea.

Inverness became a centre for the distribution of ammunition to the Grand Fleet, and for this purpose a new branch from the station to the harbour was constructed under rather exceptional circumstances. The line was proposed early in 1915, and the Highland Railway undertook to complete it in six weeks. No more was heard of the scheme until in the middle of May a message was received that the work must be started at once, as trains carrying ammunition had already been dispatched from the south! The chief engineer undertook to carry out the task in a fortnight and, assisted by 100 men from the Royal Engineers, he kept his promise. The new line was so far completed in ten days that the first of the waiting trains was able to use it.

Letters and parcels to and from the Grand Fleet were also concentrated at Inverness. To accommodate this heavy traffic, a special shed was built on the station premises, and additional accommodation was subsequently provided in part of the laundry belonging to the Station Hotel. The mails were first sorted on the train between Perth and Inverness, and placed in bags bearing the names of the ships to which they were to go. Subsequently, the sorting carriage was put on at Edinburgh. On arrival at Inverness, fresh bags for the post offices at the various Naval bases were made up. From the bases the bags were sent to the ships concerned.

The huge influx of goods traffic did not by any means represent the whole of the extra burden thrown upon the Highland Railway. Following the adoption of the north of Scotland and the Orkneys as Naval bases, large and increasing numbers of officers and men had to be carried to and from London and elsewhere. This traffic was naturally irregular, and depended on fleet movements, leave, or other conditions. For some time attempts were made to spread it over a number of trains, but this arrangement was not a success, and the whole position threatened to become chaotic.

At length, it was decided to run a special Naval train every weekday in each direction, between London (Euston) and Thurso. The train made its first journey on February 15th, 1917, and continued to run until April 30th, 1919. Until May 20th, 1917, it ran from Carlisle to Perth non-stop, via the Caledonian Railway, but after that date it was diverted over the Waverley route of the North British Railway to Edinburgh, and reached Perth via the Forth Bridge. This alteration enabled men for Rosyth Dockyard to reach their destination without changing. The journey of 717 miles from London to Thurso was covered in $21\frac{1}{2}$ hours. In the reverse direction the time was 22 h. 20 m. The train ran 272 miles over the Highland Railway in $10\frac{1}{2}$ hours (approx), including a wait of 30 m. at Inverness for meals. North of Inverness stops were made at Alness and Invergordon for passengers, and at Helmsdale and Forsinard for locomotive purposes. The up train left Thurso at 11.45 AM throughout the year. In the opposite direction London was left at 6 PM in the summer and 3 PM in the winter. The earlier departure during the winter months enabled embarkation at Thurso to be completed during daylight.

The special usually consisted of 14 vehicles, although on occasions it was run in two or three parts. Sleeping accommodation was provided for officers. The train was made up entirely of corridor stock, and the travelling master-at-arms thus had

easy access to all coaches. Certain compartments were converted into prison cells for Naval prisoners who had outstayed
their leave, or who were guilty of other offences. The number of
prisoners on the train might be anything up to 35.

When the length of the journey is taken into consideration,
the record of punctuality is high. On Sunday, January 13th,
1918, the north-bound special became stuck in a deep snow-
drift near Scotscalder and there was no early prospect of
getting it free again. Next morning the 300 passengers abandoned the train and tramped across the snow to Thurso, a
distance of 8 miles. So deep were the drifts, and so severe the
weather, that a week elapsed before the line had been sufficiently cleared for normal traffic to be resumed. Meantime,
the specials terminated at Invergordon, whence the men
proceeded by sea to Scapa Flow.

In addition to the regular Naval special, many extra troop
and Naval specials were required. At Invergordon alone,
between August 1914 and August 1919, no less than 1,020
special trains, in addition to Naval ambulance trains, were
dealt with.

Quite early in the war the north of Scotland received the
unwelcome attentions of enemy spies. Two of them, a man and
a woman, were arrested in the Station Hotel at Inverness,
thanks to the vigilance of the staff. They were taken to London
for trial and convicted. It was no doubt owing to experiences
such as these that in August 1916, Inverness and the whole
of the country to the west and north were declared a special
military area. Railway passengers who arrived at Inverness
without a permit were not allowed to leave the station or
continue their journeys to places beyond. In the same way,
Naval ratings or civilians proceeding to the Grand Fleet had
to be identified by the senior Naval officer's staff before they
were allowed to go farther.

The entry of the United States of America into the war
brought a heavy extra traffic to the Highland Railway. It was
decided to lay a huge minefield, known as the Northern
Barrage, from the Orkneys to the Norwegian coast, a distance

of over 230 miles. The United States were to supply the materials, which were to be shipped to the north of Scotland in parts, and assembled there ready for use. The work of assembling and laying the mines was to be carried out by American Naval ratings, and two bases were set up, one at Inverness, and the other at Dalmore, near Invergordon.

The two bases were known as 'US Naval Base 18' and 'US Naval Base 17', respectively. The former was situated near the Muirtown Basin of the Caledonian Canal, about a mile from Inverness. Stores and workshops were erected nearby, and the Highland Railway's canal branch was commandeered by the Admiralty, and greatly extended. The American staff was housed in the adjacent Glen Albyn Distillery. Material for this base was brought across the Atlantic to the western end of the Canal, at Corpach, where it was transhipped into lighters and conveyed through the canal to Muirtown.

At Dalmore, another distillery was requisitioned. In this case it was converted into workshops and stores, the staff being accommodated in hutments close by. Work on the new base was started in January 1918, and the first mines arrived in the following May. There was at first no pier available, and the mines had to be sent by rail to Invergordon, 4 miles distant, largely by means of an extra line, laid beside a public road. The construction of a pier was begun in July 1918, but it was not finished until after the Armistice had been signed. In 1919 it proved exceedingly useful when the Northern Barrage was being dismantled.

Material for Dalmore was landed at Kyle of Lochalsh, and sent thence by train. Ships from America arrived about once per fortnight, and three or four special trains were then worked daily for about a week. Because of the heavy gradients and sharp curves between Dingwall and Kyle, loads were restricted to 11 wagons each. The whole railway west of Dingwall, together with the pier at Kyle, was commandeered by the Admiralty. The Highland Railway was allowed to run one train each way for passengers and mails, but all goods traffic for the Isle of Skye and the Outer Hebrides by this route was

INVERNESS.

The Highland Railway Company's
STATION HOTEL.

*Patronised by their Royal Highnesses the Prince and Princess of Wales,
the Duke of Cambridge Prince and Princess Christian,
and other Members of the Royal Family, and by most of the Nobility of Europe.*

This Large and Handsome Hotel, adjoining the Station, with all the modern Improvements, and elegantly Furnished, is acknowledged to be one of the best appointed in the Kingdom. Has recently undergone extensive Additions and Alterations, and contains numerous Suites of comfortable and lofty Apartments. A new elegant Coffee-room, Drawing-room Smoking and Billiard-rooms, Lavatories, and Bath rooms.

Pianos are at the free disposal of the occupants in every Private Sitting-room.

Parties leaving in the morning can go over the grand Scenery along the Skye Railway, or visit either Loch-Maree, Gairloch, Dunrobin, or Golspie, and return the same day to the Hotel.

Table d'Hôte at 6.30 and 7.30; on Sundays at 5 p.m. only.

AN OMNIBUS ATTENDS THE STEAMERS.
HOTEL PORTERS ATTEND AT THE STATION.
POSTING

TARIFF:

SITTING-ROOMS—Ground Floor, per Day	5s	
Do. —1st Floor	7s 6d to 10s	
BEDROOMS—1st ,,	3s 6d	
Do. —2nd ,,	3s 0d	
Do. —3rd ,,	2s 6d	
If two Persons occupy one Bed, 1s extra.		
BOARD—Plain BREAKFASTS & TEAS.	1s 6d	
Do., with Cold Meat or Broiled Ham	2s	
Do., with Chops or White Fish,	2s 6d	
Do., with Salmon, Steak, or Ham and Eggs, or Chicken with Ham and Tongue	3s	
TABLE D'HÔTE BREAKFAST	3s	

LUNCHEONS and SUPPERS—Cold Meat	1s 6d	
Soup	1s and 1s 6d	
DINNERS—From the Joints	2s 6d	
Soups, Fish, Entrées, &c., &c., as per daily bill of fare, at proportionately moderate charges.		
TABLE D'HÔTE	4s 6d	
SPECIAL DINNERS in Private Sitting-Rooms from	5s	
A large assortment of choice WINES as per List.		
FIRES—Sitting-room, 1s 6d; Bedroom, 1s.		
BATHS—Hot, 1s 6d; Cold, 1s; Hip or Sponge, 6d.		

SERVICE—A charge of 1s 6d per day will be made to Visitors occupying Rooms. In other cases, 3d per Meal.

A Large Comfortable Room is provided for Commercial Gentlemen.

EDWARD CESARI, Manager.

Gracious living as advertised in the timetable of July 1885

stopped. Whatever was sent had to be worked by sea from Glasgow.

The Company's hotels also played their part in the struggle. At the Station Hotel in Inverness scenes of great activity were witnessed. Prior to the provision of Naval barracks, many ratings who had arrived in Inverness too late to complete their journey the same day were accommodated on hastily-made-up shakedowns on the floor. Later on, officers and men travelling by the Euston–Thurso Naval special were provided with a meal during the short time that the train waited at the station. There were occasions when the numbers catered for approached 1,000 in a single day.

At Kyle of Lochalsh, the hotel was taken over and used for officers and quarters in connexion with the work of the senior Naval officer for the district. The hotel at Dornoch was used first by the Gordon Highlanders, while they were in training in the district, and later by the Canadian Forestry Corps. To provide hospital accommodation for the American Naval ratings on service in this country, the Strathpeffer Hotel was commandeered.

The Highland was a comparatively small railway, and the task of those responsible for its operation was beset with peculiar difficulties. Of the 272 miles of main line between Perth and Thurso, only about 47 were double track (including the $7\frac{1}{4}$ miles from Perth to Stanley Junction), although there was the alternative route from Aviemore to Inverness, via Forres. Nor was the system well provided with sidings. On the outbreak of the war the Company possessed only 75 miles. Between Perth and Inverness, both of which are practically at sea level, the trains have to surmount one summit of 1,484 ft, and another of 1,315 ft, by means of long and severe gradients. On the northern main line, the railway reaches a height of 484 ft above sea level, near Lairg, and of 708 ft, near Forsinard.

Under pre-war conditions the traffic was only heavy during the summer. The bulk of the necessary repairs to the track and rolling stock were carried out during the rest of the year. The

Company's stock of locomotives, carriages and wagons was limited, although it sufficed for all normal needs.

Such, in brief, was the system that was suddenly called upon to handle a vastly increased traffic, and it is not surprising that the Company soon found itself in serious difficulties. The continuous heavy work since August 1914 rendered it impossible to carry out the usual programme of locomotive repairs during the winter. By the summer of 1915, partly for this reason, and partly on account of the excessive strain to which they were subjected, locomotives were constantly breaking down. In August of that year, out of 152 engines owned by the Company, 50 had had to be withdrawn from service, and 50 others were in urgent need of repairs. Nor was it possible to remedy these deficiencies. Many of the Company's engine-fitters had been called up for service, and there were not enough left to carry out repairs. Engines sent to repairing firms in the south were detained for long periods for like reasons. Not only was important Government traffic seriously delayed, but there was every prospect of a complete failure.

An appeal was made to the Railway Executive Committee, and a meeting took place, at Perth, between the locomotive superintendent and the chief engineer of the Highland Railway, and the mechanical engineers of certain other railways. As a result, it was decided that 20 locomotives should be loaned to the Highland by other companies; that any fitters that could be spared from other railways should be released for temporary employment at Inverness; and that representations should be made to the War Office with a view to securing the return of certain Highland fitters then serving with the Forces. The efforts to obtain extra skilled labour failed completely, but the additional engine power proved invaluable.

A year later the situation again became acute. Three crossing loops, between Perth and Inverness, had been closed for lack of signalmen. The main line was badly congested with special traffic, while many of the regular trains had to be run in duplicate, or even triplicate. Nineteen engines were still on loan, but 42 of the Company's own locomotives were undergoing repairs. To these difficulties was added another, in the form of a serious shortage of wagons. Ordinary and special goods traffic had greatly increased, and the various forestry camps in the Highlands were responsible for a large and growing timber traffic.

An appreciable measure of relief was afforded by diverting a large amount of goods traffic for the south over the Great North of Scotland Railway, via Keith and Aberdeen, but this arrangement by no means solved the problem, and a number of wagons were hired from certain Scottish and English Companies. In February 1918, 150 additional 12-ton coal wagons were secured from the South Eastern & Chatham Railway for carrying the American mines from Kyle of Lochalsh. These trains were hauled by engines supplied by the London & South Western Railway.

By the summer of 1918 the Highland Railway had 850 wagons on loan, but notice had been given that 700 of these would be required by their owners in the early autumn. As the result of further appeals to the Railway Executive Committee, it was arranged that 1,150 wagons should be loaned to the Company (in addition to those specially reserved for the Kyle of Lochalsh traffic).

Nor did the advent of peace at once relieve the Highland of its difficulties. There was a progressive decline in Naval and military traffic, but the timber traffic continued to be exceptionally heavy. The position was also complicated by the resumption of holiday traffic in the summer of 1919.

Had it not been for the Government control, and the existence of the powerful Railway Executive Committee, the Highland Railway would have been faced with an impossible task during the war years. Fortunately, as part of a temporarily unified national railway system, it was able to rely for help on its larger partners. It was this fact alone that enabled the Company to avoid the complete breakdown that would have been little short of a national disaster.

Out of a staff of approximately 3,000 in August 1914, no less than 756 served with the fighting forces in the course of the next four years, and 87 made the supreme sacrifice. A memorial to the fallen was placed on the wall of the head offices in the Station Square at Inverness, and unveiled on August 6th, 1921, by General Lord Horne.

SOME NOTABLE ACCIDENTS

Throughout its history, the Highland Railway enjoyed an exceptional freedom from serious accidents. Minor mishaps there were in plenty, but until the year 1894 it stood to the Company's credit that no accident had been fatal to a passenger. In that year there was a collision, resulting in one death. Many years passed by, and then, in 1914, came a second disaster in which several passengers lost their lives. But it must be admitted that the circumstances were exceptional, and could not have been foreseen.

The opening ceremony of the Inverness & Nairn Railway, in November 1855, was marred by an alarming incident. A young man riding in one of the open trucks of the special train incautiously leaned over the side of the vehicle and struck his head against the abutment of a bridge. Fortunately his injuries, although serious, did not prove fatal.

As an instance of the rather slipshod methods of early railway working, on May 6th, 1856, as a passenger train from Nairn to Inverness was approaching the terminus, it was diverted, without warning, on to the harbour branch and came into collision with some loaded wagons. Several passengers were bruised and shaken. It transpired that after the passage of the wagons on to the branch, the points had not been reset for the main line, to allow the train to enter the station.

Shortly after the opening of the line to Keith, the unfinished state of the Spey viaduct at Orton (see Chapter Two), together with unauthorized procedure, gave rise to an accident at Mulben. On September 4th, 1858, the last train of the day (the 4.45 PM from Inverness) had been hauled over the bridge by means of ropes, and was waiting, on the east side, for the engine to take it on to Keith. The driver backed on to his train somewhat too hard, with the result that the special brake van, attached at the rear of all trains between Elgin and Keith, because of the steep gradients on either side of the Spey viaduct, was derailed. Efforts to re-rail the van failed, and it was finally decided to let the train proceed to Keith, on the understanding that the driver should return with the engine to pick up the vehicle. The stationmaster at Mulben, unaware of this arrangement, closed his station for the night after the train had passed and, in accordance with his instructions, set the points for a safety siding, at the head of the gradient leading down to the river.

On arrival at Keith, the driver shunted the coaches into a siding, and set out to pick up the derailed van. With him, on the engine, were his fireman, the guard of the train, and three engine cleaners, who wished to return to their homes. The engine was diverted, without warning, into the siding at Mulben, and derailed at the buffer stops. The three cleaners were killed, and the guard and fireman seriously injured. The primary responsibility was found to rest with the driver and guard, who had returned along the main line without seeking authority, or without warning the stationmaster at Mulben.

Failure to take adequate precautions with a heavy train led to a collision at Pitlochry on October 21st, 1865. The 12.40 PM passenger train from Inverness to Perth was approaching the station, when the brakes proved insufficient, and the train ran past the platform, and came into sidelong collision with a down train, which was just arriving. The latter sustained considerable damage, and nine passengers were injured. The inspecting officer drew attention to the necessity for an adequate reserve of brake power on a line abounding in steep gradients, and suggested that at stations where trains were booked to cross, one should be brought to rest before the other was allowed to approach the crossing loop.

It would appear, however, that some six years later the traffic arrangements were still far from perfect. On November 9th, 1871, a collision occurred at Dava, in which five persons were injured. A heavy passenger train required assistance in the rear up the long bank to the summit, but the bank engine was not attached while the coaches were at rest. Instead it was sent in pursuit, after the train had left, with the result that it came into violent collision with the rear vehicle. At the inquiry, the Board of Trade inspector stressed the undesirability of bank engines following moving trains.*

Nor were the regulations governing single-line working always strictly observed. On November 11th, 1872, an up goods train from Tain to Inverness arrived at Novar, where it was booked to cross the down mail train. In defiance of the regulations the stationmaster allowed the goods train to draw forward to pick up some sacks of potatoes, which had been stacked beside the line. Before it could return to the crossing loop, the passenger train arrived, and a collision took place in which eight persons were injured.

Within a few days of the opening of the railway to Wick and Thurso, a rather curious mishap occurred near Altnabreac, on August 6th, 1874. Torrential rain had fallen for some hours, and the sides of a shallow cutting were badly washed away. As the early-morning train from Wick to the south was approaching, a mass of rock, about 1½ tons in weight, fell across the track. The engine and the first two vehicles were completely derailed, but the passengers escaped with a shaking.

An accident that might have had very serious results occurred on November 26th, 1885, at The Mound, where the line runs for some distance close to the seashore. An up mixed train, made up of 11 wagons and seven passenger vehicles, was approaching the station, when an axle on one of the leading wagons broke, and the whole train was derailed. The engine and several wagons ploughed along the track for about 500 yds before coming to rest, but the remainder of the train, including the passenger coaches, ran down the embankment and fell in the sea. There were several passengers on the train, but all escaped with a shaking and a wetting.

*This practice was not confined to the Highland. It was allowed for some years on other railways.

The year 1886 was remarkable for a series of mishaps to mixed trains. In each case the goods wagons were marshalled in front of the passenger coaches, a practice contrary to the recommendations of the Board of Trade. On May 24th, a train consisting of 40 wagons and two passenger coaches was descending the incline between Dava and Forres when one of the rear vehicles ran off the road. The engine and the leading wagons continued in safety, but the remainder of the train was derailed. A few days later, on June 1st, another derailment, due to a broken axle, took place between Golspie and Brora. In this case, the train consisted of 34 goods wagons and two passenger coaches marshalled in the rear. The third mishap occurred on September 28th, between Mulben and Keith, with a short train. None of these accidents resulted in more than slight injuries to passengers.*

In his report, the Board of Trade inspecting officer drew attention to the undesirability of placing wagons in front of passenger coaches on mixed trains. Not only did it deprive the driver of his continuous brake, but in each of the above cases the derailment was due to a wagon running off the road. The passengers would have suffered no ill-effects had the marshalling been reversed.

The railway Company replied that it was unable to adopt the Board's recommendations, as this would necessitate the removal of the passenger coaches before shunting operations could be carried out, and the trains would suffer considerable delay.

An unusual accident occurred on October 14th, 1892, at Achnashellach, on the Dingwall & Skye Railway. When the afternoon mixed train from Dingwall arrived, the engine was detached to do some shunting, the weight of the coaches overcame the resistance of the brake in the rear van, which was out of order, and the whole train ran back down a steep gradient. It came to rest some distance up the succeeding rise, whence it moved forward once more towards the station.

*The Company was not always so fortunate. In a similar mishap between Kingussie and Kincraig, on August 2nd, 1888, six persons were injured.

Although darkness had fallen, the engine was sent back to pick up the train. It had proceeded some distance when it met the runaways moving in the opposite direction, and a violent collision ensued in which eight passengers were seriously injured. The primary responsibility for the accident was found to rest with the guard and driver, who should not have allowed the engine to be uncoupled until the train was adequately braked. The stationmaster was also severely censured for sending the engine in pursuit of the runaways, before he had ascertained their exact whereabouts.

The Regulation of Railways Act of 1889 brought the question of mixed trains to a head. Under the Act, the Board of Trade issued an order to the Highland Railway on February 16th, 1891, requiring all passenger vehicles on mixed trains to be marshalled next to the engine, so that the continuous brake might work on them. On more than one occasion the time given to the railway Company in which to comply with the order was extended, and it was not until January 1st, 1896, that it came into force. It would appear, however, that some 18 months later the regulations were not always observed, and correspondence passed between the Board of Trade and the Company.

On September 20th, 1897, the general manager stated that in future trains would comply with the order. Five days later, however, a mixed train was allowed to leave Dingwall for Strome Ferry with four passenger coaches attached in the rear. Near Raven's Rock Summit a coupling broke between two goods wagons, and the ten rear vehicles began to run back down the steep incline. Gathering speed, they overcame the brake in the guard's van, and it was not until they had covered nearly 6 miles, and crashed through the gates of a level crossing, that they could be brought to rest, some 200 yds from the junction with the main line. Fortunately, there was no derailment, and the passengers escaped unhurt. The mishap was due to the failure of a faulty coupling on another company's wagon, and could not have been prevented, but the inspecting officer pointed out that the passenger coaches need not have been involved had the marshalling been reversed. The Company's representative stated that following the occurrence the Board of Trade order had been enforced.

On August 2nd, 1894, a collision occurred at Newtonmore in which one passenger was killed and eight other persons seriously injured. The 11.50 AM passenger train from Perth to Inverness was booked to cross an up goods train at Kingussie, but on that day it was running late, and the goods train was allowed to proceed to Newtonmore. For some reason which was never satisfactorily explained, the points at the south end of the station were left set for the up crossing loop, but the down home signal was, of course, locked in the 'on' position. Unfortunately, the down distant signal was defective, and had remained at 'all clear' after the passing of the previous train. The driver of the passenger train observed this signal and, expecting a clear road, approached the station at the usual speed. The train overran the home signal, and collided head-on with the engine of the goods train.

Amongst the passengers was Professor Dobbie, of Edinburgh, who was taking one of his horses by train to Inverness. From Perth to Blair Atholl, the professor had travelled in an ordinary compartment, in the centre of the train, but wishing to feed the animal, he alighted at that station, and travelled thence in the horsebox, marshalled next to the engine. This change cost him his life, because the leading vehicle bore the brunt of the collision.

By a curious coincidence, this same train was involved in the most serious accident that ever occurred on the Highland Railway. Soon after noon on June 18th, 1914, a terrific thunderstorm broke in the hills near Carr Bridge, on the direct line to Inverness. Swollen by torrential rain, the waters of the Baddengorm Burn, which passes under the railway close to the station, rose to an abnormal height. The arch of the bridge became blocked with tree trunks and other debris, with the result that the water became 20 ft deep and 170 ft wide on the upstream side, and the foundations of the bridge were undermined.

When the train reached the bridge, the structure had partially collapsed, but the damage was not apparent from the footplate. The subsidence of the track threw the tender of the engine off the road, and the train came to rest on the bridge. The extra weight of the coaches caused the complete collapse of the arch, and the train was thrown down the bank. The middle passenger coach fell into the raging torrent, and was submerged. Five passengers were drowned, and nine others injured.

It was stated at the enquiry that the bridge had been solidly built and well maintained. Every reasonable allowance had been made for sudden floods, but the storm was exceptionally severe. The flood had even demolished the century-old road bridge a short distance upstream and had swept away many tons of soil from the adjacent farm lands. The disaster was due to the scouring effect of the water seeking an outlet, after the arch had become blocked. A new bridge, with an even more generous allowance for flood water, was erected in the remarkably short space of three weeks. Meanwhile, all traffic had to be sent via Forres.*

THE SNOW FIEND

Although the north of Scotland enjoys the advantages of an insular climate, and its extremes of cold are still further tempered by the genial influence of the Gulf Stream, the advent of winter frequently brings heavy falls of snow. It seldom happens, however, that the weather is uniformly severe throughout the country, and a raging blizzard may sweep Sutherland and Caithness, while on the Grampians the snow is comparatively light. In the same way the moors of Ross-shire may escape lightly, when deep drifts are accumulating in the uplands of Moray. As a general rule, storms are more severe in the east than in the west.

*A similar cloudburst occurred on July 8th, 1923, at almost the same point. In this case, the material damage was far greater, and the line was closed for some weeks. Fortunately no train was involved.

Fortunately, avalanches are rare in the Highlands, and in no case are conditions near a railway suitable for their occurrence. On the other hand, serious difficulties frequently arise through deep drifting.

A snowfall of quite moderate depth, if accompanied by a high wind, can pile up in drifts several feet thick. And the wind frequently blows the already deposited snow across open country until it encounters some obstacle – such as the side of a railway cutting – against which it can accumulate.

The Inverness & Nairn and Inverness & Aberdeen Junction Railways passed through comparatively low-lying country, where the risk of serious drifting was reduced to a minimum, but it was otherwise with the direct line to Perth, which crossed high mountains, and bleak, open moorlands, affording little, if any, protection from the fury of the storm. In the spring of 1864, after the railway had been open for seven months, the engineer reported that, although there had been several sharp storms, no serious trouble had arisen. In February 1865, however, snow fell heavily throughout the north of Scotland, and communication between Perth and Inverness was only restored with difficulty after the line had been closed for five days. It was realized that special precautions were necessary to guard against deep drifting.

It was decided to erect artificial barriers, known as 'snow fences', beside the railway at the most vulnerable points. The fences were built up from old sleepers, set upright in the ground, like a palisade.* A careful study of local conditions determined the direction from which the worst drifting usually occurred, and for that reason the fences were not always parallel to the track. The snow accumulated on the weather side of the fence, leaving the lee side more or less clear. Experience showed that one line of fencing was not always sufficient, and a second, or even a third, line was provided in certain cases. Sometimes fences were needed on both sides of the line.

*At some points, mounds of earth were made to serve the same purpose.

North of Inverness, on the borders of Sutherland and Caithness, a special type of fencing, known as a 'blower', the invention of a Lancashire man named Howie, was tried with some success. Close-boarded fences, very similar to long wooden tables, were erected on both sides of the track, much closer to the rails than the ordinary snow fences. The inner edges of the blowers almost touched the ground, but the outer edges were raised some eight or ten feet. These artificial troughs deflected the wind currents away from the railway, causing the snow to be swept up and deposited on the far side, out of harm's way.*

To preserve the lines of communication intact during severe storms, telegraph poles were placed in the most sheltered positions possible. Point rods were encased with wood, and signal wires were carried on high posts.

Although the snow fences afforded a large measure of protection, deep drifts calling for the use of snowploughs were common. The earliest ploughs were designed by William Stroudley, and were of three types, to suit varying conditions. So successful did they prove that those built subsequently were generally similar. At the beginning of the winter many engines were fitted with a small or nose plough, similar to a cowcatcher, attached to the front buffer beam. The running of the engine was not impeded in any way, and if necessary two engines could be coupled together. Engines so fitted were used for hauling trains, and were capable of overcoming drifts up to 2 ft in depth. If the depth of snow was between 2 and 5 ft, a pilot engine fitted with a somewhat larger plough was attached to the train. The third and largest type of plough extended to the top of the smokebox of the engine, and was used for clearing the line of drifts of 10 or 12 ft. Three or four engines were coupled together, and the plough charged at full speed into the snow from a distance of about half a mile.

*On the Burghead branch, where the line ran some miles beside the shore of the Moray Firth, blowers were used to clear the line of drifted sand.

If the engines were unable to force their way through the drift, they had to be dug out, and the line cleared by manual labour, a task rendered the harder if the line was in a deep cutting, as the snow had first to be thrown part of the way up the slope, whence a second, or even a third, gang of men lifted it clear over the top. Often an accumulation of ice in the flange-ways threw the snowplough engines off the road, and it was no easy matter to get them re-railed.

Whenever a heavy fall of snow was expected, the station-masters along the line were instructed to wire reports of local weather conditions to Inverness. These telegrams were remarkable for their brevity, and, although they might vary considerably, usually mentioned the state of the wind (a matter of the utmost importance). A typical selection would read as follows:

'Fair and calm.'

'High wind, but little snow.'

'Snowing heavily, but little wind.'

'Heavy snow, wind rising.'

'Bad drifts. Trains should be piloted and loads reduced where possible.'

'Blizzard raging. No trains should be run unless preceded by snowplough engines.'

Long experience had shown the staff at headquarters exactly how to act on the receipt of such information. But the telegraph wires were liable to break under the weight of the snow, and outlying stations were isolated.

A close watch was kept on certain well-known danger spots, and none gave rise to greater anxiety than Dava Moor, where the drifts frequently defied the efforts of the ploughs, with the result that the train service was temporarily suspended. On more than one occasion trains were completely buried, after being abandoned. Scarcely less notorious were the windswept heights on either side of Druimuachdar Summit, where a cutting some 3 miles north of Struan, known as the Black

Tank, earned an evil reputation. The doubling of the railway over the mountains effected a marked improvement on this section, as the wider space between the banks gave the snow less chance to accumulate.

The bleak, exposed moors on the borders of Sutherland and Caithness have been aptly termed 'The Country of the Snow Drifts'. Between Helmsdale and Georgemas, the railway ran through the heart of this district, and serious blocks were common. One particularly bad spot, near Altnabreac, was known as the Fairy Hillocks, a name suggestive of anything rather than trouble of this kind. As was the case at Dava, trains were buried on more than one occasion.

Fortunately it was not every winter that was memorable for its severe storms, although it was but seldom that the ploughs were idle throughout the season. During six consecutive winters, from 1866 to 1871, and again from January to March 1875, heavy snowfalls were experienced throughout the Highlands. The snowplough engines kept the line open with great difficulty, and many trains were seriously delayed. In January 1868 a sudden thaw caused extensive flooding, and the railway was severely damaged in several places. By way of contrast, the winters of 1876 and 1877 were remarkable for their mild weather and absence of snow.

The arctic conditions which prevailed throughout the winter of 1880–81 were long remembered. On December 17th a train became snowbound some distance south of Dava station, and had to be abandoned. The passengers managed to reach the shelter of the station before the storm increased to an intensity that would have rendered escape impossible. The train was completely buried, and when at last it was located, the snow had accumulated to a height of 60 ft above the coaches. An up train, carrying passengers and five trucks of cattle, shared a like fate on the other side of the station. The passengers made good their escape, but the cattle were not so fortunate. Despite desperate efforts to liberate them, the animals refused to leave the shelter of the trucks, and perished by suffocation. In after years, the men who laboured so heroically yet unavailingly to avert this catastrophe, recalled with reluctance the frenzied bellowings of the stricken beasts, who seemed conscious of the disaster that was overtaking them. A relief train, hurriedly dispatched to the scene of the block, was itself lost for some time.

One month later, on January 17th, the whole country was swept by a terrific blizzard, which paralysed communications far and wide. By the 21st, two trains were buried in the snow, north of Helmsdale, and the southern main line was blocked at Dava and Druimuachdar. Telegraphic communication was completely interrupted, and on the following day a slight collision occurred, near Forres, between a snowplough engine and a passenger train. Traffic was resumed between Inverness and Perth on the 23rd, but the north line was not cleared until the 24th. For some days the service was very uncertain, and many trains were delayed.

Traffic on the Caithness line was again brought to a standstill on February 7th, although the ploughs succeeded in forcing a passage through the drifts within 24 hours. But the respite was of short duration, for on the 13th a blizzard swept over the Highlands which disorganized the whole system for three days. Thurso and Wick were isolated, and some of the drifts on the Perth line were upwards of 200 yds in length and 25 ft deep.

Further storms occurred early in March, and deep drifts accumulated at several points. Between Grantown and Forres a long length of telegraph wires collapsed under the weight of the snow, and the greater portion of the southern main line was completely cut off from headquarters. On the morning of the 3rd, Thomas Robertson, the superintendent, and a telegraph clerk, John Menmuir, travelled by train from Inverness to Grantown, via Elgin and the Speyside branch of the Great North of Scotland Railway, whence they made their way on horseback to a snowed-up train åt Huntly's Cave, 2 miles south of Dava. There a wire was tapped, an instrument was placed in circuit, and for the time being crossing orders and instructions were issued from a carriage of the train.

Even more severe and long-continued were the snow blocks of 1894–5. A severe blizzard on December 29th was followed by a succession of heavy storms in January and February, and the last of the drifts on the Highland Railway was not cleared away until March 4th. During some of this period all sections of the main line from Perth to Wick were snowbound, except the 100 miles from Inverness to Helmsdale. A regular service, suffering no more than slight delays, was worked between these points, although on more than one occasion the snowploughs had difficulty in keeping the line clear near Lairg. The Dingwall & Skye Railway was abandoned completely, while every effort was made to re-open the main lines.

The winter herring season was in full swing, and serious delays were experienced in getting the fish through from Wick to the south. One of the first trains to be snowed up was a fish special, which was completely buried near the Fairy Hillocks, after being hastily abandoned. When it was relieved, ten days later, the contents were delivered to their destinations in perfect condition. The snow had acted as a gigantic refrigerator.

Gangs of men laboured unceasingly to clear the line, and when the drift had been reduced to about a mile in length, an attempt was made to get the mails through by carrying them over the blocked section to a train waiting at the south side. Some gentlemen, who had been held up in Thurso, asked leave to accompany the party and, at length, received permission to do so 'at their own risk'. That the journey was of unusual interest, although somewhat hazardous, may be judged by the following extract from a letter written by one of them some days later:

In the cold grey of the early morning we travelled in the van, getting various tips from the platelayers and Post Office men as to the best way of getting through the deep snow. The chief of these was to tie your trousers tightly round your boots with stout string, which you brought round under your boots, like a stirrup. Thus equipped, a line of men, each with a mail-bag over his shoulder, followed by six passengers, struggled through the deep snow. If you did not break through the crust, it was all right; if you did, you went down three or four feet, and had to drag your legs up as best you could. It was very picturesque to come upon one hundred men working in the snow in that lonely spot, looking like silhouettes against the white. The men were in triple tier, and each spadeful had to be handled three times before it reached the top.

Towards the end of January the line was cleared, and several fish specials were worked through to the south. Two days later a gale, accompanied by heavy snow, sprang up in the opposite direction and reblocked the cuttings in a single night! The position was now much worse. The passage of the ploughs had made deep artificial cuttings in open places, and the height of the natural cuttings had been increased by the snow thrown out over the sides. The arduous task of digging had to be begun all over again, rendered the harder by the height through which the snow had to be lifted before it could be thrown clear, and by further falls of snow. Meanwhile, deep drifting had occurred farther south, at Dava and Druimuachdar. The ploughs had been constantly at work, and on more than one occasion traffic had been brought to a complete standstill.

Twelve years later came the Christmas blizzard of 1906. On December 28th conditions were exceptionally severe. The north mail was snowed up at Ardullie, near Foulis, and great difficulty was experienced in getting it dug out. Deep drifts accumulated on the Skye line at Achterneed, and traffic was suspended for three days.

Exceptionally deep drifts were again experienced in January 1918, on the moors of Caithness. On the 13th a snowplough engine, sent to clear the line for the Euston–Thurso Naval special, became completely stuck in a drift near Scotscalder, and the special itself was snowed up a few hours later a short distance to the south. A relief train, carrying a party of 100 men, including 50 Naval ratings and men taken from urgent Government work at Kyle of Lochalsh, was hastily dispatched to the scene of the block, but so severe was the weather that a week elapsed before the line had been sufficiently cleared for the full service to be resumed.

CHAPTER ELEVEN

LOCOMOTIVES AND ROLLING STOCK

WILLIAM BARCLAY: 1855–65

IN READINESS for the opening of the Inverness & Nairn Railway, William Barclay was appointed locomotive superintendent. He continued in this position after the Company had been amalgamated with the Inverness & Aberdeen Junction Railway. A native of Montrose, Barclay was a nephew of Alexander Allan, formerly of the London & North Western Railway, and well known as the inventor of the straight link valve motion. His engines were similar in design to those built at Crewe under the supervision of his uncle.

The locomotive works were established beside the passenger station at Inverness, on a site formerly occupied by a small sheet of water known as Loch Gorm. The buildings were surrounded by a triangle of lines formed by the approaches to the two parts of the passenger station, and the connecting spur, or Rose Street curve. Subsequently, separate carriage and wagon shops were erected on a piece of land known as Needlefield, lying to the north of the through line.

The first locomotive class introduced by Barclay consisted of four 2–2–2 tender engines which were built by Hawthorns, of Leith, between 1855 and 1857. As the Inverness & Nairn Railway was isolated from all other railways, the engines were taken by sea from Leith to Inverness. They bore numbers 1 to 4, and were named after residences of directors: No 1, *Raigmore*; No 2, *Aldourie*; No 3, *St Martin's*; No 4, *Ardross*.

They had outside-cylinders, 15-in diameter by 20-in stroke, 6-ft driving wheels, and 3 ft 6 in carrying wheels. The boiler carried two safety valves, and was domeless. Originally the only protection for the engine men was a small, plain weather-board. The tenders ran on four wheels. Nos 1 and 2 were the only two engines delivered to the Inverness & Nairn Railway, the remaining pair being built for the Inverness & Aberdeen Junction Railway. For some time they worked the whole of the passenger and goods traffic.

Nos 1 and 2 were rebuilt as 2–4–0s by William Stroudley about the year 1869. The additional pairs of wheels were re-moved from Nos 3 and 4 which were scrapped. At the same time No 2 was provided with a large boiler, and the cylinders were enlarged to 15½-in diameter by 22-in stroke. As rebuilt the engines weighed 27½ tons, but details of their weights when new have not survived. No 1 was scrapped a few years later, but No 2 worked until 1899.

Two more singles, Nos 12 and 13 (named *Belladrum* and *Lovat* respectively), were built by Hawthorns in 1862 for working the Inverness & Ross-shire Railway. They were generally similar to those already described, but they had 16-in by 22-in cylinders, and were fitted with cabs. No 12 was rebuilt as a 2–2–2 tank engine in 1871, and put to work on the Aberfeldy branch, where it remained until 1879, named *Breadalbane*. It was reconditioned, fitted with a dome, and renamed *Strathpeffer* in 1885, and worked the branch from Dingwall to the spa for some time, being finally withdrawn in 1898. No 13 was not converted. In 1874 it was renamed *Thurso* and sent to work the branch from that town to Georgemas Junction. It was scrapped in 1890.

In 1863 and 1864 a further series of 2–2–2 passenger locomo-tives appeared, the first two being built by Hawthorns, and the remainder by Neilson & Co. They had 17-in by 22-in cylinders, and 6 ft 1½ in driving wheels. Except for a few minor differences they were similar to the earlier series of engines, but had generally increased dimensions. The weight in working order was 31 tons. The tenders ran on six wheels and weighed 24 tons. The names and numbers were:

(*Top*) Tank engine No 17 as originally built

(*Bottom*) Inverness & Nairn Railway locomotive No 1, *Raigmore*,
as built in 1855

BUILT BY HAWTHORNS OF LEITH

No	Name		Renamed
28	Glenbarry	...	Grantown
29	Highlander	...	Forres

BUILT BY NEILSON & CO

No	Name		Renamed
30	Prince*	...	—
31	Princess*	...	—
32	Sutherland	...	Cluny
33	Atholl	...	Birnam
34	Seafield	...	Perthshire
35	Kingsmills	...	Isla Bank
46	Clachnacuddin	...	Kingussie
47	Bruce	...	(1) Lovat; (2) Beauly
48	Cadboll	...	Dingwall
49	Belladrum	...	Helmsdale
50	Aultnaskiah	...	Badenoch
51	Caithness	...	Blair Atholl
52	Dunphail	...	—
53	Stafford	...	Golspie
54	Macduff	...	—
55	Cluny	...	(1) Sutherland; (2) Invergordon

*These names were bestowed in honour of the Prince and Princess of Wales (afterwards King Edward and Queen Alexandra), who were married in 1863.

All except No 32 of this class were converted into 2–4–0s by David Jones between 1872 and 1892. Their cylinders were enlarged (not in all cases at the time of their conversion) to 18-in diameter by 24-in stroke, and the weight in working order increased to 36 tons. Seven of them were reboilered between 1881 and 1896, and at the same time were fitted with tyres which increased the diameter of the driving wheels to 6 ft 3 ins. After this last alteration they weighed 37½ tons in working order. The remainder of this class, which did not receive new boilers, were scrapped between 1897 and 1900. The others survived for some years longer, and No 35 lasted until the grouping as No 35A.

The first locomotives designed solely for goods traffic were a series of seven 2–4–0s, built by Hawthorns in 1858 and 1859. Their chief dimensions were: cylinders 16 ins by 22 ins, coupled wheels 5 ft diameter, boilers 10 ft 9 ins long by 4-ft diameter, and weight in working order 28 tons. The tenders ran on four wheels and weighed 16 tons. As there was still no through railway to the south, these engines were delivered by sea to Lossiemouth, and reached the Inverness & Aberdeen Junction Railway via the Morayshire Railway. The names and numbers of this class were:

No	Name		Renamed
5	*Seafield*	...	*Tain*
6	*Bruce*	...	*Helmsdale*
7	*Fife*	...	*Dingwall*
8	*Altyre*	...	*Beauly*
9	*Aultnaskiah*	...	*Golspie*
10	*Westhall*	...	*Duncraig*
11	*Stafford*	...	*Skibo*

Between 1873 and 1875, Nos 7 and 10 were fitted with bogies for working on the Dingwall & Skye Railway. Their cylinders were enlarged to 17 ins by 24 ins, and the weight increased to $32\frac{1}{2}$ tons. At the same time they were provided with Jones' standard chimney and cab. Renaming took place at the time of these alterations, but the names were removed later. The remainder of the class were fitted with standard chimneys and cabs between 1875 and 1880, and had their cylinder stroke increased to 24 ins. The whole series was scrapped between 1893 and 1899.

Two more 2–4–0s, Nos 14 and 15, were built by Hawthorns in 1862. They were slightly larger than the earlier goods engines, and were fitted with cabs. They weighed $30\frac{1}{2}$ tons in working order. Subsequently they were fitted with 5 ft $2\frac{1}{2}$ in wheels and 17-in by 24-in cylinders. No 15 was scrapped in 1893, and at the same time No 14 was renumbered 6. It was withdrawn from service (after being renumbered 49) in 1901. Originally these locomotives were named *Loch* and *Sutherland* respectively. No 14 was renamed *Evanton*, and No 15 became successively *Dunkeld* and *Foulis*.

Two further series of ten 2–4–0 goods engines were built by Sharp, Stewart & Co in 1863 and 1864 respectively. The two sets were generally similar, both having cylinders 17-in diameter by 22-in stroke, 5 ft 1½ in coupled wheels, and boilers 4 ft 1 in in diameter. The second set differed from the first in having longer boilers, larger fireboxes, and a greater wheelbase. The weights in working order were 32 and 33 tons respectively. The first set were numbered 18 to 27, and the second 36 to 45.

The numbers and names of the two series were as follows:

No	Name		Renamed
18	Inverness	...	—
19	Dingwall	...	Golspie
20	Birnam	...	—
21	Forres	...	—
22	Aviemore	...	—
23	Murthly	...	Dalcross
24	Invergordon	...	Lairg
25	Novar	...	—
26	Beauly	...	—
27	Conon	...	—
36	Nairn	...	—
37	Struan	...	—
38	Kincraig	...	—
39	Aviemore	...	—
40	Keith	...	—
41	Kingussie	...	—
42	Lentran	...	—
43	Dava	...	—
44	Brodie	...	—
45	Dalcross	...	—

With the exception of No 24, which retained its second name (*Lairg*) until the end, all these locomotives had their names removed before they were withdrawn from service. It appears that both No 22 of the earlier series and No 39 of the later entered service with the name *Aviemore*. Unless confusion has arisen in following the vagaries of Highland Railway renaming, the most probable explanation is that No 22 became nameless a few months after it was built.

Both series were rebuilt by Jones between 1874 and 1893, with domed boilers and flush-topped fireboxes. The cylinders were enlarged to 18-in diameter by 26-in stroke, and the diameter of the driving wheels was increased to 5 ft 3 ins by means of thicker tyres. Standard cabs were fitted and the weights were increased by 1 ton. No 22 was withdrawn from service in 1896, and most of the others shared a like fate within the next few years, but three veterans (Nos 27, 37 and 42) survived until the grouping.

In 1862 the Inverness & Aberdeen Junction Railway took over the Findhorn Railway, and with it a small 0-4-0 tank engine which had been purchased by that Company from Neilson & Co. It had a square saddle tank extending to the front of the smokebox, 12-in by 16-in cylinders, and cast-iron wheels 3 ft 6 ins in diameter. A peculiarity of the design was that the valves were operated by means of gab motion, rendering the engine incapable of working expansively. Later, Stroudley discarded this motion in favour of standard Stephenson link motion. While in the service of the Findhorn Railway the engine was not designated by either name or number, but it became No 16 on the books of its new owners. In 1872 it was sold to Hector Mackenzie of Wick, and used on the construction of the northern section of the Sutherland & Caithness Railway. Subsequently it performed similar work in the south of Scotland.

For working the Burghead branch a small 0-4-0 tank engine, with 4-ft wheels, was purchased from Hawthorns in 1863, numbered 17, and named *Hopeman*. It had inside cylinders, 13-in diameter by 18-in stroke, and was the first inside-cylinder engine possessed by the Company. The boiler had a raised firebox, and a plain weatherboard was the only protection afforded to the enginemen. The side-tanks were raised above the footplate, and extended to the front of the smokebox. Owing to the considerable overhang at the trailing end, the engine proved unsteady, and a pair of wheels, 3 ft 1 in in diameter, was added by Stroudley. The weight in working order then became 20 tons.

In 1879 it was replaced on the branch by a more powerful engine, and became successively goods yard pilot at Forres, and carriage works shunter at Inverness. After this second change of duty, the number was removed, and the engine was named *Needlefield*. A cab was fitted, and the original chimney replaced by one of Jones' standard design. Subsequently it was converted into a stationary engine for driving the saw-mill at Lochgorm works, but in 1898 it was renovated, numbered 1A, and set to work again as a shunting engine. It remained on this duty until it was sold in 1902.

On May 31st, 1865, Barclay resigned his position of locomotive superintendent at Inverness, and took over the management of an hotel in Liverpool. Some time later he returned to railway work, under Samuel Johnson, at the Stratford works of the Great Eastern Railway. After that he became locomotive superintendent to the Thetford & Watton Railway, but relinquished that position in 1878 to re-enter the service of Johnson, who had joined the Midland Railway. He died a few years later.

While Barclay was at Inverness, the engines were painted dark green, with black borders and bands, without any lining. The numbers were painted on the buffer beam.

WILLIAM STROUDLEY: 1865-9

Barclay's resignation coincided with the formation of the Highland Railway, and his successor thus became that Company's first locomotive superintendent. The choice of the directors fell on William Stroudley, works manager at the Cowlairs shops of the Edinburgh & Glasgow Railway. Born in 1833, in Oxfordshire, Stroudley had secured wide experience with railway companies and private firms before taking up his duties at Inverness.

The only locomotives built for the Highland Railway to

Stroudley's designs were three small o–6–o saddle-tank engines, which were turned out from Lochgorm works in 1869, 1873 and 1874. They had 14-in by 20-in inside-cylinders, 120 lb per sq in boiler pressure, and 3 ft 7 in wheels. The boilers were 7 ft 9¼ ins long and 3 ft 7 ins in diameter. The weight in working order was 23½ tons. The class is interesting historically both on account of being the first constructed at the Company's works, and as the prototype of the well-known 'Terriers', introduced by Stroudley on the London, Brighton & South Coast Railway. The engines were numbered and named as follows:

No		Name
56	...	*Balnain*
57	...	*Lochgorm*
16	...	*St Martin's*

No 56 was the only one completed while Stroudley was at Inverness. The remaining two were built after Jones had become locomotive superintendent. No 16 replaced the Findhorn engine after the latter had been sold.

No 56 was rebuilt by Jones in 1895, and Nos 16 and 57 by Peter Drummond two years later. The alterations consisted of substituting larger boilers, fitting thicker tyres to increase the diameter of the wheels to 3 ft 8 ins, and providing a bunker of increased capacity. These changes brought the weight up to 26 tons.

In 1899, No 16 was named *Fort George*, and sent to work on the branch to that place when first opened. Two years later it was renumbered 49. No 56 was named *Dornoch* in 1902, and was the first engine to work on the Dornoch Light Railway. The three engines were still in service when the Highland became part of the LMSR in 1923.

Stroudley resigned at the end of 1869 in order to take up a similar appointment on the London Brighton & South Coast Railway. He remained at Brighton until his untimely death in December 1889. He introduced on the Highland Railway the style of painting which was afterwards so well known to the

South Coast. Passenger engines were yellow, with crimson framing and elaborate lining. For goods engines a dark green livery was adopted. The names were painted in gilt letters on the driving splashers or side-tanks, and the number plates were oval, with raised brass figures on a vermilion ground.

DAVID JONES: 1870–96

Stroudley was succeeded by David Jones, his chief assistant. Born in Manchester in 1834, Jones had served his apprenticeship under John Ramsbottom, at the Longsight shops of the London & North Western Railway. In November 1855 he entered the service of the Inverness & Nairn Railway, and was appointed assistant locomotive superintendent three years later. For a short time after Barclay's resignation, Jones was in charge at Lochgorm, but on the appointment of Stroudley he reverted to his former position for another four years.

The first locomotive to be built to the designs of Jones was a 4–4–0, which appeared in 1874. It was named *Bruce*, and was intended for working main-line passenger services. It had outside-cylinders, 18-in diameter by 24-in stroke, 140 lb per sq in boiler pressure, and 6 ft 3 in coupled wheels. The boiler was 10 ft 8½ ins long and 4 ft 2 ins in diameter. The engine weighed 42 tons in working order, of which 27 tons rested on the driving wheels. The design embodied several features which afterwards became standard on the Highland. These included the curious double chimney, its outer casing fitted with louvres which, by inducing a strong upward current of air, were intended to assist in forcing the draught, and to lift the exhaust well clear of the cab windows. The safety valves were placed transversely on the firebox casing, and the cabs were of unusual design, with rounded corners and square fronts. The tenders weighed 30 tons, and were of rather small capacity. They ran on six wheels. Ten engines of this class were built by Dübs & Co, of Glasgow, in 1874. Numbers and names were:

No	Name		Renamed
60	*Bruce*	...	*Sutherland*
61	*Sutherlandshire*	...	*Duke*
62	*Perthshire*	...	(1) *Stemster*; (2) *Huntingtower*;
			(3) *Ault Wharrie*
63	*Inverness-shire*	...	*Inverness*
64	*Morayshire*	...	*Seafield*
65	*Nairnshire*	...	*Dalraddy*
66	*Ross-shire*	...	*Ardvuela*
67	*The Duke*	...	*Cromartie*
68	*Caithness-shire*	...	(1) *Caithness*; (2) *Muirtown*
69	*The Lord Provost* ...		(1) *Sir James*; (2) *Aldourie*

Between 1876 and 1888 seven more engines of this class were constructed at Inverness:

No	Date New	Name		Renamed
4	1876	*Ardross*	...	*Auchtertyre*
71	1883	*Clachnacuddin*	...	—
72	1884	*Bruce*	...	*Grange*
73	1885	*Thurlow*	...	*Rosehaugh*
74	1885	*Beaufort*	...	—
75	1886	*Breadalbane*	...	—
84	1888	*Dochfour*	...	—

No 4 was renumbered 31 in 1899, and 31A in 1911. Between 1897 and 1900 Drummond rebuilt Nos 60, 61, 62, 66, 67, 68 and 69 with new boilers having a pressure of 150 lb per sq in.

Although somewhat handicapped by their small tenders, these engines performed a vast amount of useful work. They all remained in service until 1907, but at the end of 1922 only Nos 67, 72, 74, 75 and 84 survived. By that time they had all passed on to the 'A' list.

In 1877 two 2–4–0 passenger engines were built at Lochgorm works. They had 16-in by 22-in outside-cylinders, and 6 ft 3 in coupled wheels. The boilers were 9 ft 5½ ins long and 4 ft 1 in in diameter. The working pressure was 140 lb per sq in. They weighed 35 tons, of which 23 tons was available for adhesion. The tenders weighed 27 tons.

These engines were numbered 1 and 3, and replaced the

older locomotives similarly designated. They were named *Raigmore* and *Ballindalloch* respectively. These names were retained throughout their existence, but the numbers were changed to 29 and 30 respectively in 1898. The latter was scrapped in 1910, but No 29 (renumbered 29A) lasted until 1912. They were never rebuilt.

Jones' next class consisted of three 2–4–0 tank engines, built in 1878 and 1879 for branch-line services and shunting. Their cylinders and fireboxes were the same size as those of the 2–4–0 tender engines, built in 1877, but the boilers were slightly shorter. They had 4 ft 9 in coupled wheels, and weighed 36 tons in working order. The whole of this class were built in the Company's works, and received the following numbers and names:

No		Name
17	...	*Breadalbane*
58	...	*Burghead*
59	...	*Highlander*

Soon after they appeared they were rebuilt with a leading bogie, because trouble was experienced with the single leading axle. No 17 was renamed *Aberfeldy* in 1886, and renumbered 50 in 1901. All three survived (on the 'B' list) until the grouping, and were latterly used for shunting.

The satisfactory results obtained with the two converted 2–4–0 engines on the Dingwall & Skye Railway induced Jones to build the well-known 'Skye Bogie' class for working that section of the Highland Railway. They were generally similar to the 4–4–0 main-line engines, but differed in certain details. They had 5 ft 3 in driving wheels, and 150 lb per sq in boiler pressure. The weight in working order was 43 tons, of which 28 tons was available for adhesion. The tenders weighed 30 tons. Nine of this class were built at Lochgorm works:

No		Date New
70	...	1882
85	...	1892
86	...	1893

No		Date New
87	...	1893
88	...	1895
5	...	1897
6	...	1897
7	...	1898
48	...	1901

Contrary to usual Highland Railway practice, none of them received names. The last four were not completed until after Jones had resigned. In consequence they were fitted with Drummond's standard type of chimney.

In 1899, Nos 5, 6 and 7 became Nos 32, 33 and 34 respectively. Between 1903 and 1907, No 48 worked on the Invergarry & Fort Augustus Railway. The whole of the class was still in active service at the end of 1922.

A further series of 4–4–0 tender engines for main-line services was constructed during 1886 by the Clyde Locomotive Co Ltd, of Glasgow. They were the first engines to be built by this firm, which was later taken over by Sharp, Stewart & Co, and renamed the Atlas works. They differed from the previous series in having shorter boilers, 9 ft 9½ ins long, and longer fireboxes. The boiler pressure was 160 lb per sq in, and the weight in working order 43 tons. They were provided with tenders of increased capacity, weighing 31½ tons. Eight of this class were constructed:

No	Name		Renamed
76	*Bruce*	...	—
77	*Lovat*	...	—
78	*Lochalsh*	...	—
79	*Atholl*	...	—
80	*Stafford*	...	—
81	*Colville*	...	—
82	*Fife*	...	*Durn* (this name was removed in 1916)
83	*Cadboll*	...	*Monkland*

No 76 was sent to the Edinburgh Exhibition of 1886 before being placed in service. None of these engines had been

(*Top*) Inverness & Aberdeen Junction Railway 2–4–0 goods
engine No 36, built in 1864

(*Bottom*) Side elevation and plan of Pullman sleeping-car

withdrawn when the Highland lost its separate identity in 1923, although all had passed on to the 'A' list.

To replace the old single-wheeled tank engine, No 12, on the Strathpeffer branch, Jones designed a small 0–4–4 saddle-tank engine specially for this service, which was built at Inverness in 1890. It was numbered 13 and named *Strathpeffer*. It had inside-cylinders, 14-in diameter by 20-in stroke, and 4 ft 3 in coupled wheels. The boiler was 3 ft 6½ ins in diameter, and the weight in working order was 32 tons.

In 1901 this locomotive was rebuilt at Inverness with side-tanks and a new boiler of Drummond's design. The adhesion weight was slightly reduced, although the total weight was increased to 34 tons. It had previously been renumbered 53. Two years later it was renamed *Lybster*, and sent to work on the Wick & Lybster Light Railway, where it remained until the grouping.

The next addition to the stock was a series of 4–4–0 tender engines for main-line passenger services, constructed in 1892 by Neilson & Co. They were merely an enlargement of Jones' standard designs, having similar cylinders, wheels and motion, but larger boilers, 9 ft 9½ ins long by 4 ft 6 ins in diameter, and carrying a steam pressure of 160 lb per sq in. The weight, in working order, was 45 tons, of which 29½ tons rested on the coupled wheels. This series was known as the 'Strath' class, and consisted of 12 engines, all in service in December 1922:

No	Name		Renamed
89	*Sir George*	...	—
90	*Tweeddale*	...	*Grandtully*
91	*Strathspey*	...	—
92	*Strathdearn*	...	*Glendean*
93	*Strathnairn*	...	—
94	*Strathtay*	...	—
95	*Strathcarron*	...	—
96	*Glentilt*	...	—
97	*Glenmore*	...	—
98	*Glentruim*	...	—
99	*Glentromie*	...	—
100	*Glenbruar*	...	—

In 1892 the Highland Railway purchased from Dübs & Co two 4–4–0 outside-cylinder side-tank engines, which had been built for the Uruguay Eastern Railway, but which had not been delivered owing to some financial hitch. They became Nos 101 and 102 on the books of the Highland Railway. With the exception that the cowcatchers and the American pattern head-lights were removed, the engines were delivered practically as built. They had 16-in by 22-in outside-cylinders, 5 ft 3 in driving wheels, and carried 140 lb per sq in working pressure. The weight in working order was 41 tons 12 cwt. It was thought that the covers over the side bars would prove useful on the Burghead branch, where heavy sand drifts occur, but they were soon dispensed with because it was impossible to get at the cross heads without removing the covers.

In the following year three more 4–4–0 tank engines were built by Dübs & Co. They were slightly heavier than the two previous engines, and had standard Highland Railway fittings, but were otherwise similar. They were numbered 11, 14 and 15. In 1899, No 11 was renumbered 51, and in 1900, Nos 14 and 15 became 50 and 52 respectively. In the following year No 50 was again altered to 54. In 1906, No 102 was rebuilt by Drummond with his standard chimney and boiler mountings.

These engines proved exceedingly useful on branch lines. For many years they ran to Burghead, Fortrose, Portessie and Aberfeldy. No 52 worked on the Invergarry & Fort Augustus Railway while that line was under the management of the Highland Railway. The whole of the class survived until the grouping.

The year 1894 witnessed the introduction of Jones' famous bogie goods engines, the first 4–6–0s to work on a British railway. The design was a radical departure from existing practice, and every credit is due to Jones for the bold way in which he broke with long-established tradition by introducing an entirely new wheel arrangement. The class comprised 15 engines, all built by Sharp, Stewart & Co. They were numbered 103 to 117 inclusive.*

*No 103 is preserved at Glasgow Museum of Transport.

At the time of their construction, they were undoubtedly the most powerful main-line engines in the country. They had 20-in by 26-in outside-cylinders, 5 ft 3 in coupled wheels, and 175 lb per sq in boiler pressure. The boilers were 13 ft 9 ins long by 4 ft 7⅞ ins in diameter. The weight in working order was 56 tons, of which 42 tons were available for adhesion. The tenders had six wheels and weighed 38 tons 7 cwt. Although intended for hauling goods trains, they also did good work with passenger services. The whole of the class passed into the hands of the LMSR in 1923.

The last series of engines designed by Jones were 15 large 4–4–0s, which appeared from the works of Dübs & Co in 1896. Considerably more powerful than any which had hitherto worked on the Highland Railway, they were among the foremost in the country as regards tractive effort at the time of their construction. They had 19-in by 24-in outside-cylinders, 6 ft 3½ in coupled wheels, and 175 lb per sq in boiler pressure. The boilers were 10 ft 6¾ ins long by 4 ft 4⅞ ins in diameter. The weight in working order was 47 tons, of which 29 tons 19 cwt rested on the coupled wheels. The tenders were identical with those of the 4–6–0 goods engines. These engines were known as the 'Loch' class:

No		Name
119	...	*Loch Insh*
120	...	*Loch Ness*
121	...	*Loch Ericht*
122	...	*Loch Moy*
123	...	*Loch an Dorb*
124	...	*Loch Laggan*
125	...	*Loch Tay*
126	...	*Loch Tummel*
127	...	*Loch Garry*
128	...	*Loch Luichart*
129	...	*Loch Maree*
130	...	*Loch Fannich*
131	...	*Loch Shin*
132	...	*Loch Naver*
133	...	*Loch Laoghal*

Mention must be made of the engines owned by the Duke of Sutherland. When the railway was extended from Golspie to Helmsdale, the third Duke purchased a small 2–4–0 tank engine from Kitson & Co, of Leeds. For the time being it worked a passenger service from Dunrobin to the temporary station at Gartymore, near Helmsdale, but as soon as the extension was linked up with the main line from Inverness it was reserved for hauling the Duke's private coach, and kept at Brora. As delivered to the Duke, it was named *Dunrobin*, and had outside-cylinders 10-in diameter by 18-in stroke, and coupled wheels 4-ft diameter. The weight in working order was 21 tons.

On the death of the Duke in 1892, his son decided to have a more powerful engine for his own use. Three years later Jones designed, and Sharp, Stewart & Co built, an 0–4–4 side-tank engine, with 13-in by 18-in inside-cylinders, and 4 ft 6 in coupled wheels. Like its predecessor, it was named *Dunrobin*, and was painted dark green, with black bands and yellow lines. For the accommodation of the Duke and his friends while riding on the footplate, a seat with leather cushions, extending the full width of the cab, was provided over the bunker. On the front weatherboard were inscribed the names of several illustrious travellers who inspected the engine while guests of the Duke. In 1896 a new shed was built for the engine at Golspie.

The original *Dunrobin* passed to the Highland Railway, who sent it to Sharp, Stewart & Co for rebuilding in 1896. A new and larger boiler was provided, the cylinders were increased to 12-in diameter by 18-in stroke, and the side-tanks were extended halfway along the boiler barrel. The weight in working order was increased to 24 tons. On its return it was numbered 118, named *Gordon Castle*, and sent to work the branch from Orbliston Junction to Fochabers. Subsequently it was renamed *Invergordon* and used for shunting at Invergordon Harbour. During the war it was lent to the Great North of Scotland Railway, but it was still on the books of the Highland Railway at the end of 1922. It was sold to a contractor shortly after the grouping.

On October 31st, 1896, as the result of an accident while testing a new engine, David Jones was forced to resign his position, after 48 years of railway life, 41 of which had been spent at Lochgorm works. Some time later he left the north of Scotland for London, where he died in 1906 in his 73rd year.

Jones continued Stroudley's style of painting for some years, but afterwards adopted black, lined with red and white, for goods engines. In 1885 radical changes were made in the livery, which became standard for all locomotives. Save for the framing, which was dark crimson with a black border and yellow and red lines, the engines were painted a pea green with a border of a darker shade, black bands, and red and white lines. The buffer beams were painted like the framing, but had a vermilion panel in the centre. The Stroudley pattern number plates were retained.

PETER DRUMMOND: 1896–1912

To fill the vacancy occasioned by the retirement of David Jones, the directors chose Peter Drummond. A native of Ayrshire, Drummond had served his apprenticeship with Forrest & Moor, of Glasgow. In 1870 he joined the London Brighton & South Coast Railway under Stroudley, but returned to Scotland some years later to enter the service of the North British Railway. Eventually he joined his elder brother, Dugald, on the Caledonian Railway, and became works manager at St Rollox, the position he was holding at the time of his appointment to the Highland in November 1896.

The first locomotive class designed by Drummond was a series of 20 4–4–0 passenger engines, known as the 'Small Bens', which were named after mountains in the Highlands. Eight were built by Dübs & Co in 1898 and 1899. These were followed between 1899 and 1901 by nine others, constructed at Lochgorm works, and the remaining three came from the North British Locomotive Co of Glasgow in 1906:*

*The North British Locomotive Co was formed in 1903 by an amalgamation of Sharp Stewart & Co, Dübs & Co and Neilson Reid & Co.

No	Name	Date New		Makers
1	*Ben-y-Gloe*	1898	...	Dübs & Co
2	*Ben Alder*	1898	...	,,
3	*Ben Wyvis*	1898	...	,,
4	*Ben More*	1899	...	,,
5	*Ben Vrackie*	1899	...	,,
6	*Ben Armin*	1899	...	,,
7	*Ben Attow*	1899	...	,,
8	*Ben Clebrig*	1899	...	,,
9	*Ben Rinnes*	1899	...	Highland Railway
10	*Ben Slioch*	1899	...	,,
11	*Ben Macdhui*	1899	...	,,
12	*Ben Hope*	1900	...	,,
13	*Ben Alisky*	1900	...	,,
14	*Ben Dearg*	1900	...	,,
15	*Ben Loyal*	1901	...	,,
16	*Ben Avon*	1901	...	,,
17	*Ben Alligan*	1901	...	,,
38	*Ben Udlaman*	1906	...	North British Loco Co
41	*Ben Bhach Ard*	1906	...	,, ,,
47	*Ben a' Bhuird*	1906	...	,, ,,

The design of these engines represented a complete departure from previous Highland Railway standards, and resembled very closely Dugald Drummond's practice on the North British and Caledonian Railways. They had 18¼-in by 26-in inside-cylinders, and 6-ft coupled wheels. The boilers were 10 ft 6 ins long by 4 ft 6¼ ins in diameter, and carried a steam pressure of 175 lb per sq in. Drummond further adhered to his brother's standards by mounting the safety valves on the dome. In 1920 they were moved to a separate mounting above the firebox. The weight of the engine in working order was 46 tons, of which 31 tons 4 cwt rested on the driving wheels. The tenders also embodied the usual Drummond characteristics. They ran on six wheels, and weighed 37½ tons. Subsequently, four of the class were fitted with eight-wheel tenders.

These engines were slightly smaller than the 'Loch' class, and were seldom called upon to undertake the heaviest duties on the southern main line. They usually worked north of Inverness, and to Keith. During the time that Highland

engines were working through to Aberdeen the trains were
frequently hauled by an engine of this class.

In 1900 six goods engines of entirely new design were introduced. They were of the 0–6–0 type with inside-cylinders, and
were built by Dübs & Co. They had 5-ft wheels, and their
boilers and cylinders were interchangeable with the 'Small
Bens'. The weight in working order was 43 tons. As delivered
by the makers, they were provided with eight-wheeled tenders,
weighing 40 tons, but these were subsequently exchanged for
four six-wheel tenders belonging to the 'Small Ben' class, and
two similar ones, originally supplied to the 'Big Bens', which
appeared in 1908.

In 1902 four more 0–6–0 engines were built by Dübs & Co.
They differed from the previous series in having water-tube
fireboxes. The class was completed five years later by the
addition of two further engines, with normal fireboxes, built
by the North British Locomotive Co. The whole of these
engines built after 1900 were supplied with six-wheeled tenders when new. The 12 engines of this class were built:

No	Makers		Date New
134	Dübs & Co	...	1900
135	,,	...	1900
136	,,	...	1900
137	,,	...	1900
138	,,	...	1900
139	,,	...	1900
18	,,	...	1902
19	,,	...	1902
20	,,	...	1902
21	,,	...	1902
36	North British Loco Co	...	1907
55	,, ,,	...	1907

A series of six 4–6–0 passenger engines which were considerably more powerful than the existing 4–4–0 classes were
built by Dübs & Co in 1900. Four others followed from the
same firm in 1902; and the North British Locomotive Co
added two more in 1910 and 1911. They had 19½-in by 26-in

outside-cylinders, and 5 ft 9 in coupled wheels. The boilers were 14 ft 4½ ins long by 4 ft 9¾ ins in diameter, and carried 180 lb per sq. in steam pressure. The safety valves were mounted over the firebox. The weight in working order was 58 tons 17 cwt, of which 43 tons 17 cwt rested on the coupled wheels. They were provided with large tenders, weighing 38 tons 2 cwt, running on two four-wheeled bogies. These engines were known as the 'Castle' class; their numbers and names were:

No	Name		Date New
140	*Taymouth Castle*	...	1900
141	*Ballindalloch Castle*	...	1900
142	*Dunrobin Castle*	...	1900
143	*Gordon Castle*	...	1900
144	*Blair Castle*	...	1900
145	*Murthly Castle*	...	1900
146	*Skibo Castle*	...	1902
147	*Beaufort Castle*	...	1902
148	*Cawdor Castle*	...	1902
149	*Duncraig Castle*	...	1902
30	*Dunvegan Castle*	...	1910
35	*Urquhart Castle*	...	1911

They were primarily intended for working heavy traffic between Perth and Inverness, a task that they accomplished with conspicuous success. It was not until May 1913 that one of them worked through to Wick.

In 1910, No 146 took part in some comparative trials with a North British Railway 4–4–0, No 867, each engine hauling a train of eight bogie coaches, a saloon and a brake van. On the Highland Railway the trials took place between Blair Atholl and Dalwhinnie, and on the North British Railway over the steeply-graded section between Perth and Kinross. In 1912, No 141 was fitted with a Phoenix superheater, but the experiment did not prove successful, and the apparatus was removed.

Following the introduction of the 'Castle' class, Drummond turned his attention to tank engines, of which the Highland Railway stood in need. In 1903 and 1904, three 0–6–0 shunting

THE HIGHLAND RAILWAY

LOCOMOTIVE ✦ DEPARTMENT

No. Special

PASS TO RIDE ON LOCOMOTIVE ENGINE

INVERNESS, 18th Sept 1907.

Issued to *Mr Gairns*

Available *Inverness & Kyle of Lochalsh.*

P. Drummond Loco. Supt.

N.B.—Before this Pass can be used the Holder must sign the declaration on back.

tank engines were built at Lochgorm works. They had 18-in by 24-in outside-cylinders, and 5 ft 2½ in wheels. Their boilers were 10 ft 4 ins long by 4 ft in diameter, and the working pressure was 160 lb per sq in. The weight in working order was 47½ tons. The wheels and boilers had previously been used on older engines which had been withdrawn from service. This class was numbered 22, 23 and 24. These engines were followed by some small 0–4–4 tanks for branch-line services. Built at Inverness in 1905 and 1906, they had 14-in by 20-in outside-cylinders and 4 ft 6 in coupled wheels. The boilers were 8 ft 2 ins long by 3 ft 10¼ ins in diameter, and the safety valves were mounted on the dome. The weight in working order was 35¾ tons. The class consisted of four engines:

No	Name		Date New
25	*Strathpeffer*	...	1905
40	*Gordon Lennox*	...	1905
45	—	...	1905
46	—	...	1906

Six 4–4–0 tender engines, known as the 'Big Bens', were built by the North British Locomotive Co in 1908 and 1909. They were generally similar to the 'Small Bens' differing only in having larger boilers, 5 ft 3 in diameter, a steam pressure of 180 lb per sq in, and separate mountings for the dome and safety valves. The weight in working order was 52 tons 6 cwt, of which 35 tons 4 cwt rested on the coupled wheels.

The tenders of the first four were originally of the standard six-wheel pattern, weighing 38 tons 7 cwt, but two of them were subsequently supplied with eight-wheel tenders weighing 41 tons 14 cwt at the time of their construction:

No	Name		Date New
61	*Ben na Caillich*	...	1908
63	*Ben Mheadhouin*	...	1908
66	*Ben Mholach*	...	1908
68	*Ben a' Chait*	...	1908
60	*Ben Bhreac Mhor*	...	1909
62	*Ben a Chaoruinn*	...	1909

In 1909, Nos 66 and 68 were renumbered 64 and 65 respectively. Two of the class were fitted with Smith's feed water heater in 1914, but the upkeep of this complicated apparatus proved too costly, and it was soon removed.

The last locomotive design to be introduced to the Highland Railway by Drummond was a powerful 0–6–4 tank engine, with 18¼-in by 26-in inside-cylinders and 5 ft coupled wheels. The boiler was 10 ft 6 ins long and 4 ft 6¼ ins in diameter, and the working pressure was 180 lb per sq in. The weight in working order was 69½ tons. Eight of this class were built by the North British Locomotive Co, four in 1909, and four in 1911. The first batch were numbered 39, 64, 65 and 69, and the second 29, 31, 42 and 44. Very soon after their arrival, Nos 64 and 65 were altered to 66 and 68 respectively, to provide for consecutive numbering of the 'Big Ben' class. Although primarily intended for banking purposes, they were also used for local passenger and goods trains.

In January 1912 the position of locomotive superintendent on the Glasgow & South Western Railway became vacant on the retirement of James Manson. Peter Drummond obtained the appointment and remained at Kilmarnock until his death in June 1918.

During his 15 years at Inverness, he placed more than 60 new engines in service, and almost entirely changed the character of the locomotive stock. This extended to the external appearance of the engines, all of which exhibited unmistakeable Drummond features. He modified the painting of the engines soon after taking charge, the red lining being abolished, and the black boiler and panel bands being edged with white, whilst the initials HR appeared for the first time on the tender sides or tanks, and also on the front buffer beams, together with the number. When the 'Castle' class appeared, the lettering on the tender became 'Highland Railway', but in 1903 this was altered to 'The Highland Railway'. The same year also witnessed the introduction of a new livery. The engines, including the buffer beams, were painted a plain green of darker shade, with no lining whatever. The initials and the engine number on the buffer beam were retained.

The whole of the locomotives designed for the Highland Railway by Drummond passed into the hands of the LMSR in 1923.

FREDRICK SMITH: 1912–15

Drummond was succeeded by Fredrick Smith. Born in 1872, Smith had served his apprenticeship in the Gateshead shops of the North Eastern Railway, and had been works manager at Inverness since 1903.

The first locomotives to be constructed under him were four 4–6–0s of the 'Castle' class which were built by the North British Locomotive Co in 1913. They differed from the previous engines of the class in having extended smokeboxes and deflector chimneys:

No		Name
26	...	*Brahan Castle*
27	...	*Thurso Castle*
28	...	*Cluny Castle*
43	...	*Dalcross Castle*

Shortly after it appeared, No 43 became No 29, exchanging numbers with one of the 0-6-4 tank engines.

To cope successfully with the heavy and increasing traffic between Perth and Inverness, Smith designed a large 4-6-0 tender engine, with 21-in by 28-in outside-cylinders, and 6-ft coupled wheels. Steam distribution was effected by means of Walschaerts valve gear, and the boiler, working at 170 lb per sq in, was provided with a Belpaire firebox, Robinson superheater, and Ross 'pop' safety valves. Wakefield mechanical lubricators and Smith's feed water apparatus were fitted. The weight of the engine in working order was 72 tons 6 cwt, and the six-wheel tender weighed 47 tons 7 cwt.

Six of the class were ordered from the shops of R. & W. Hawthorn, Leslie & Co, of Newcastle-on-Tyne. The first two, numbered 70 and 71, and named *River Ness* and *River Spey* respectively, were delivered in September 1915. By some extraordinary oversight the final designs had never been submitted to the chief engineer, and it was soon found that the locomotives were too heavy for the track and bridges on the Highland Railway. Their use was therefore vetoed, and a few weeks later they were sold, together with the remainder of the class, still under construction, to the Caledonian Railway. They were numbered 938 to 943 on that Company's books, and worked between Glasgow and Aberdeen. By this time the Highland Railway was experiencing considerable difficulty in handling the heavy wartime traffic owing to a serious shortage of locomotive power, and the sudden withdrawal of the eagerly-awaited new engines made the position even worse.*

Following the refusal of the chief engineer to sanction the use of his new engines, Smith resigned and, leaving Inverness, set up in practice as a consulting engineer in Newcastle-on-Tyne. During his short period of office, the external appearance of the engines underwent a further change. The number plates were removed from the cab sides, and the number was painted

---

* The bridges and track on the Highland Railway were strengthened after the grouping, and the former 'River' class engines were able to work between Perth and Inverness.

in large gilt figures higher up, while a small aluminium number plate with raised figures was fixed to the smokebox door. A somewhat lighter green was adopted, still without any lining, and except in the case of some of the more recent express engines, which were green all over, the boilers were plain black.

CHRISTOPHER CUMMING: 1915-22

The directors chose Christopher Cumming to replace Smith. Cumming had served an apprenticeship in the shops and drawing office of the North British Railway, and had subsequently gained experience at various locomotive depots on that system. At the time of his appointment to the Highland, he held the position of district locomotive superintendent at Burntisland. The outbreak of the war had thrown a great strain on the locomotive department at Inverness, and Cumming's first years of office were rendered exceedingly difficult on that account.

Additional locomotive power was urgently required, and the new superintendent decided, for the time being, to revert to the designs of David Jones. In 1916 an order was placed with the North British Locomotive Co for three engines of the 'Loch' class. It is a great tribute to the designer that this type should have been considered suitable for new engines after the lapse of 20 years. Save for a few minor alterations, the new engines were similar to the series built in 1896. They were delivered in 1917 and were numbered 70 (*Loch Ashie*), 71 (*Loch Garve*), and 72 (*Loch Ruthven*).

The North British Locomotive Co also received an order for three additional engines of the 'Castle' class. They appeared in 1917:

No		Name
50	...	*Brodie Castle*
58	...	*Darnaway Castle*
59	...	*Foulis Castle*

Although generally similar to Drummond's engines, they had larger boilers, and the diameter of the driving wheels was increased to 6 ft. The weight in working order was 60 tons 13 cwt. The tenders were also of increased capacity. They weighed 40 tons, and ran on six wheels.

The first locomotives built wholly to the designs of Cumming also appeared in 1917. They were two large 4–4–0 tender engines with 20-in by 26-in outside-cylinders, fitted with Walschaerts valve gear, and 6 ft 3 in coupled wheels. The boilers were 11 ft 4⅝ ins long, and were provided with Belpaire fireboxes, Robinson superheaters, and Ross safety valves, working to a pressure of 160 lb per sq in. Lubrication was effected by means of a Wakefield mechanical lubricator. The weight of the engine in working order was 54 tons 19½ cwt. The tenders ran on six wheels and weighed 43 tons 3¼ cwt.

Both engines were constructed by R. & W. Hawthorn, Leslie & Co and were numbered and named 73 (*Snaigow*) and 74 (*Durn*) respectively. They were sent to work on the northern line from Inverness to Wick.

In the following year Cumming designed, and Hawthorn, Leslie & Co built, a series of four large 4–6–0 goods engines, numbered 75 to 78. They had 20½-in by 26-in outside-cylinders, fitted with Walschaerts valve gear, and 5 ft 3 in coupled wheels. The boilers were 13 ft 9 ins long and tapered from 4 ft 7 11/16 ins to 4 ft 6⅝ ins diameter. They were fitted with Ross safety valves, arranged for a pressure of 160 lb per sq in. The firebox was of the Belpair type, and Robinson superheaters were provided. The weight of the engine in working order was 65¼ tons. The tenders ran on six wheels, and weighed 39 tons 1½ cwt. Four more engines of this class were built by Hawthorn, Leslie & Co in 1919, and numbered 79 to 82.

For handling the increasing traffic between Perth and Inverness, Cumming designed a new class of 4–6–0 engine, embodying his standard details of outside-cylinders, fitted with Walschaerts valve gear, Robinson superheaters, Belpaire fireboxes, and Ross safety valves, working to a pressure of 170 lb per sq in. The cylinders were 21 ins by 26 ins and the coupled wheels 6 ft in diameter. The boilers were 14 ft 6 ins long, and the diameter tapered from 4 ft $9\frac{11}{16}$ ins to 4 ft $8\frac{9}{16}$ ins. The weight of the engine and tender in working order was 104 tons $6\frac{1}{2}$ cwt. The tenders ran on six wheels.

These engines were known as the 'Clan' class, and were built by Hawthorn, Leslie & Co. Four were delivered in 1919 and four in 1921:

No	Name		Date New
49	*Clan Campbell*	...	1919
51	*Clan Fraser*	...	1919
52	*Clan Munro*	...	1919
53	*Clan Stewart*	...	1919
54	*Clan Chattan*	...	1921
55	*Clan Mackinnon*	...	1921
56	*Clan Mackenzie*	...	1921
57	*Clan Cameron*	...	1921

Early in 1921, No 53 was adapted for burning oil fuel on the Scarab system. Although fairly successful results were obtained, the apparatus was later removed.

The 'Clan' class have an added interest in the light of after events. They proved to be not only the last engines designed by Cumming, but also for the Highland Railway. Early in 1922, Cumming's health suffered a complete breakdown, and he was forced to resign on March 1st of that year. He died in 1924.

Cumming modified the style of painting by returning to the all-green livery standard in Drummond's time. The buffer beams were painted red. The oval number plates on the cab sides were restored, and the initials HR reappeared on the tenders.

Cumming's resignation had been unexpected, and two months elapsed before his successor could be appointed. The choice of the directors fell on David Chalmers Urie. The son of a chief mechanical engineer on the London & South Western Railway, Urie had served his apprenticeship under his father. In 1913 he was appointed assistant works manager at Eastleigh. Two years later he became assistant locomotive superintendent to the Midland Great Western Railway of Ireland, the position he was holding at the time of his appointment to Inverness in 1922.

The Railways Act had been passed in the previous summer, and in the course of the remaining months before the grouping became effective Urie was not called upon to design any locomotives for the Highland Railway. Early in 1923 he became assistant mechanical engineer to the Northern Division of the LMSR. On December 31st, 1922, the Highland possessed 173 locomotives. All these passed to the LMSR, but 23 were soon withdrawn from service, and were not included in the complete renumbering scheme instituted by the new Company.

ROLLING STOCK

The rolling stock of the Inverness & Nairn and Inverness & Aberdeen Junction Railways adhered closely to the usual designs of the period, with few outstanding features. It ran on four wheels, and was of light construction, and of rather cramped dimensions, with flat roofs, and straight sides. A fair measure of comfort was provided in the first-class carriages, but third-class passengers had to be content with bare wooden benches.

Of particular interest were some mail vans, built by Brown, Marshall & Co in 1858, for the Inverness–Keith trains. They were 20 ft 10 ins long, and weighed 9 tons. Passengers' luggage was carried on the roof, protected from the weather only by a tarpaulin, an iron railing being provided to keep it in position. Immediately in front of the luggage space was a seat for the guard, protected by a handrail and a footboard. At a later date, when the guard no longer rode outside, side wings were added to improve his view of the line. Dogs were carried in a boot, similar to that used on stagecoaches, at one end of the van. The vehicle was fitted with Newall's chain brake, and wood-covered spring buffers.

At least one of these vans survived for many years after

being withdrawn from regular passenger services. It was latterly used as a spare tool van for the locomotive department at Perth, and was broken up in 1903. The luggage rails on the roof remained until the end.

For the time being it was decided to follow the example of the Great North of Scotland Railway and provide only two classes of carriage, first and third. However, as soon as the direct line to Perth was opened, in 1863, second-class bookings were introduced throughout the system. The standard of comfort was very little superior to that afforded to the third-class passenger, and at no time did the intermediate class become extensively patronized. It was abolished completely on May 1st, 1893.

Between 1860 and 1870 several passenger coaches and vans were added to the Company's stock. They were generally similar to those already in use, but the outside seat for the guard and the baggage space on the roof were soon dispensed with.

In readiness for the opening of the railway to Wick a large order for extra rolling stock was placed with the Metropolitan Carriage & Wagon Co. The new coaches differed but little from those already described, save that they were slightly larger and heavier. They were 27 ft 6 ins long by 7 ft 4 ins wide, and weighed 9½ tons. The third-class coaches accommodated 50 passengers in five narrow compartments, with very small windows. The second- and first-class compartments were wider and offered proportionately better accommodation. A curious feature of the design was that the doors were hung with the handles on the left and the hinges on the right of a person standing facing the coach, a reversal of usual practice. Several of these coaches continued in service for more than 30 years. Latterly they were relegated to minor branches and special trains for fish workers.

A year or two later a great advance in comfort was achieved when a number of six-wheel coaches, weighing about 15 tons, appeared. The first-class coaches seated 16 passengers in four compartments, the two inner ones being provided with lavatories, while those at the ends were of the coupé type, with a seat on one side only. The latter did not prove popular, especially with summer tourists. Although they afforded an ample prospect of the end of the coach in front, the side view was no better than, if as good as, that from an ordinary compartment because of their extreme narrowness. The third-class coaches were far more economical from the railway Company's point of view. They carried 50 passengers in five compartments, and were not provided with lavatories. Oil lamps were used for lighting in both classes, and steam heating was still a dream of the future.

The first eight-wheel coaches appeared in 1878, in the form of three first-class sleeping-cars. Each car accommodated nine passengers, and was divided into two single-berth coupés, at either end, and two larger compartments, one reserved for gentlemen, containing two upper and two lower berths, and the other reserved for ladies, containing three berths, all on the same level. A side corridor ran the full length of the coach.*

The cars were placed in service on May 1st and worked between Inverness and Perth in both directions, and between Wick and Inverness, in the up direction only. There was no down night train on the northern line. No special attendant was provided, and the guard was responsible for the comfort of the passengers. The supplementary charge was 5s per berth. South of Inverness the facility proved popular, but the Wick car was withdrawn after a few months. For many years goods vehicles were attached to the night trains, and a unique example was afforded of a mixed train conveying sleeping-cars.

In 1885 it was decided to place the sleeping-car arrangements in the hands of the Pullman Car Company, and two specially-designed vehicles, each accommodating 16 first-class passengers in upper and lower berths, were constructed at the Derby works of the Midland Railway, from parts manufactured in the United States of America and sent to Scotland. They were 33 ft 3 ins long, and weighed 16½ tons. Latterly they were fitted with four-wheel bogies, but it has been stated

*Exact details of the arrangement of the berths do not appear to have survived.

that originally they ran on six wheels. Oil lamps were used for lighting, and a Baker heater, burning coke fuel, was provided. As was usual with Pullman stock at that time, the external finish was dark brown, with gilt lining and lettering. The cars were named *Balmoral* and *Dunrobin*, and were the first Pullman vehicles supplied to a Scottish railway. The owners provided a travelling attendant, at the expense of the railway Company. The supplementary charge remained unaltered. The older vehicles were withdrawn and converted into ordinary first-class carriages.

The principal trains on the southern main line frequently included stock from other railways. Both the North British and the Caledonian companies provided coaches for the through services between Inverness and Edinburgh and Glasgow, and the leading English railways with routes to Scotland sent their own, or jointly owned, sleeping-cars and coaches through to Inverness. This cosmopolitan effect was to be seen at its best in August, shortly before the start of the grouse-shooting season. Foxwell, in *Express Trains, English and Foreign*, drew attention to the 7.50 AM express from Perth to Inverness, on August 7th, 1888. The train was of extraordinary length and weight, and included stock from no less than nine foreign railways, in addition to Highland vehicles. It has been said, with a fair measure of truth, that many of the Company's regular patrons never saw the inside of a Highland coach. North and east of Inverness, foreign stock was the exception, although certain trains on the Keith line included vehicles from the Great North of Scotland Railway.

Bogie stock became general in the years following the appointment of Peter Drummond at Inverness. Soon after taking charge he designed a number of third-class and composite coaches for main-line services. The former were 48 ft long, divided into seven compartments. The composite coaches were slightly shorter, and had two first- and four third-class compartments. In certain cases one of the latter had a seat on one side only. Lavatory accommodation was provided in both classes.

By this time gas had superseded oil for lighting, and the old-fashioned alarm bell on the tender of the engine, worked by a cord running along the eaves of the carriages, was discarded in favour of the improved system of chain communication. The new stock was steam heated and the familiar foot-warmer gradually became a thing of the past.

In 1902 a special family saloon, with clerestory roof, made its appearance. It was 48 ft 8 ins long by 8 ft 6 ins wide, and was divided into a main saloon, 22 ft long, furnished with couches and easy chairs upholstered in velvet, and a smoking compartment 8 ft long, provided with leather-covered revolving armchairs. An attendant's compartment, a lavatory and a luggage locker adjoined the main saloon.

Drummond broke with long-established practice by altering the style of painting. Previously the standard livery for passenger stock had been green, with yellow lining and lettering, but the new coaches were turned out with the upper panels painted white. The lower parts and the under frames were still green. For the time being, these colours became standard, but in 1903 it was decided to revert to an all-green livery, similar to that used for the locomotives. Some ten years later Smith abolished all lining. This alteration gave the trains a distinctly plain although not unpleasing appearance.

The Pullman sleeping-cars were withdrawn from service in 1907, when the Highland Railway decided to provide its own vehicles. The new coaches were built by Hurst, Nelson & Co, of Motherwell, to Drummond's designs. They were 50 ft long by 9 ft wide, and ran on four-wheel bogies. Oil gas was used for lighting. Contrary to usual Highland Railway practice, the external finish was varnished teak.

The number of passengers requiring sleeping accommodation had fallen off considerably, and it was no longer necessary to devote a special car to their exclusive use. Each coach had four single-berth first-class sleeping compartments, connected in pairs by inner communicating doors. The remainder of the vehicle was divided into four third-class compartments, each seating eight passengers, and one, with a seat on one side only,

seating four. An attendant's compartment adjoined the
sleeping berths, and lavatories were provided at each end of the
coach. Although a side corridor was provided, the ends of the
vehicle were not gangwayed. These composite cars were found
to be exceedingly useful and economical, especially in cases
where balance working necessitated their use on day trains.
They remained in use until the grouping.

The sleeping-cars were followed by some new third-class
coaches for main-line excursion trains. They were 46 ft 4 ins
long, and seated 50 passengers in two saloons, connected by a
short corridor. Varnished teak was adopted for the external
finish, but the innovation was not further extended. During
the First World War it was completely abandoned, and both
the sleeping-cars and the saloons were painted in the Company's standard livery.

The designs adopted by Drummond became more or less
standard and subsequent additions to the passenger rolling
stock differed but little from that already in service. Latterly,
a number of vestibuled coaches appeared, and gas lighting
gradually made way for electricity. In 1916 some new Travelling Post Office vans were built for the main-line services,
running in connexion with the postal trains on the Caledonian
Railway. They were 46 ft 8 ins long by 9 ft wide, and weighed
26 tons.

Goods vehicles call for little notice, as they present comparatively few points of interest. In addition to open and covered
wagons, and cattle trucks, there were some unusual double-
decked covered wagons used for the conveyance of sheep, an
item that figured largely in the Company's recipts. The animals
were securely penned by the iron bars forming the sides of
the vehicle. Of equal importance was the fish traffic from the
northern ports to the markets in the south, and a large stock
of wagons was reserved for this purpose.

On December 31st, 1922, the Highland Railway possessed
797 coaching vehicles, 2,718 goods wagons, and 112 service
vehicles. These figures, although small by comparison with
many other companies, stand out in sharp contrast to the five

passenger coaches and 26 goods wagons that formed the complete stock of the Inverness & Nairn Railway in November 1855.

HIGHLAND RAILWAY COMPANY.

STAFF NOTICE.

General Manager and Secretary's Office,
INVERNESS, 14th April 1884.

FACING POINTS.

In future the speed of Trains at Stations, where they are not required by the Time Bill to stop, must be reduced to 15 miles an hour when passing over Facing Points.

By order.

AND. DOUGALL,
General Manager

CHAPTER TWELVE

THE HIGHLAND RAILWAY'S STEAMSHIPS

FIRST SERVICES

THE OPENING of the Dingwall & Skye Railway in August 1870 marked the beginning of a new era in the Outer Hebrides and the Isle of Skye. Previously no railway had touched the west coast, north of the Firth of Clyde, and the islands were isolated and difficult of access. The easiest, if not the most direct, route was by ship from Glasgow.

A regular fortnightly, and later weekly, service of steamers had been established in 1851 by David Hutcheson & Co, of Glasgow, between the Clyde and Stornoway, in the island of Lewis, calling in at several of the islands, in addition to places on the mainland. In 1879 the Company's interests were acquired by the late David MacBrayne, whose name has since become a household word in the Western Highlands. Under his management the number of services was greatly increased.

The directors of the Dingwall & Skye Railway had obtained powers to operate their own boats from Strome Ferry, and two steamers, the *Jura* and the *Oscar*, were purchased in readiness for the opening of the line.

The *Jura* was an iron-screw steamer (330 tons gross), built in 1857 by Wingate & Co, of Glasgow, for the West Hartlepool Screw Steam Shipping Co, and named *Admiral Cator*. Sold in 1869 to Sloan & Co, of Glasgow, and renamed *Jura*, the vessel passed into the hands of the railway Company in the following year.

The *Oscar* was an iron-screw steamer of 341 tons gross, built in 1850 by Denny Bros, of Dumbarton. After passing through the hands of several owners, she was purchased by

Sloan & Co in 1869, and sold to the Dingwall & Skye Railway
with the *Jura*.

At first the two ships maintained a daily passenger service in
connexion with the trains between Strome Ferry and Portree,
in Skye, and a weekly service to Stornoway. But traffic returns
were unsatisfactory, and in the winter of 1870 the Portree
service was reduced, and sailings to Stornoway suspended. The
latter were restored in 1871, but were maintained during the
summer only. It was possible to reach Stornoway on certain
days by changing into Hutcheson's ship at Portree.

On November 9th, 1870, less than three months after the
opening of the railway, the *Oscar* ran aground off Applecross,
and became a total loss, fortunately without loss of life. She
was replaced in 1871 by the *Carham*, a small iron paddle
steamer, of 159 tons gross. Built in 1864 by A. & J. Inglis, of
Glasgow, this vessel had previously been employed on coastal
services from Leith, and on the Clyde. At the same time the
Company placed an order with J. & G. Thompson, of Glasgow,
for an iron-screw steamer of 347 tons gross. The new ship was
completed in 1872 and named the *Ferret*.

As soon as the *Ferret* was delivered, the *Jura* was withdrawn
from service and sold. Purchased by J. Bell, of Ayr, she traded
between Scotland and the Mediterranean for some years, but
eventually passed into the hands of a Hull firm. On February
15th, 1879, she left the Humber for Smyrna with a general
cargo. Nothing more was heard of her, but a medicine chest
and a boat were eventually picked up. It was assumed that
she came to grief on the Cross Sand, off Great Yarmouth, on
the day after leaving Hull, but her fate was never definitely
ascertained.

The service from Strome Ferry to Portree continued to be
worked by the *Carham*, relieved occasionally by the *Ferret*.
The latter ran to Stornoway once a week, in addition to making
trips up and down the coast. Subsequently it was found that
the traffic did not require two ships, and the *Ferret* was taken
out of service, overhauled on the Clyde, and advertised for
charter.

THEFT OF A SHIP

In October 1880* enquiries were made by a London firm of shipbrokers, Henderson & Co, who stated that they were acting for a Mr Smith, a relative of the First Lord of the Admiralty, who wished to take his invalid wife for a health cruise in the Mediterranean. All references proving satisfactory, a contract was signed and the first three months' charter money (£270) paid over. The ship's new purser, Mr Walker, purchased large quantities of stores in Glasgow, and the *Ferret* left the Clyde for Cardiff, where she took in coal before sailing for the Mediterranean with her passengers and new crew on October 25th.

Heavy weather was encountered in the Bristol Channel, and the ship was forced to put into Milford Haven, where she remained weatherbound for a week. As soon as the weather moderated, the *Ferret* sailed for Marseilles, and was officially reported from Gibraltar on November 11th. After that nothing was heard, and at the expiration of three months the railway Company applied for a renewal of the charter money, but without result. Enquiries revealed that the firm of Henderson & Co was non-existent, and that the rich gentleman and his invalid wife were unknown. It soon became evident that false references had been used, and that the ship had been stolen. Nor did the firms in Glasgow and Cardiff from whom stores had been obtained fare any better, as the bills given in settlement of the accounts were dishonoured when they became due three months later. To make matters worse came the startling news that some wreckage bearing the name *Ferret* had been washed up on the Spanish coast. It was assumed that the vessel had foundered in a sudden storm.

Some months passed and then came strange tidings from the Antipodes, which cleared up the mystery. A small steamer, the *India*, arrived in Melbourne, where an attempt was at once

* By this time, the Dingwall & Skye Railway had been amalgamated with the Highland Railway.

made to sell her. The suspicions of the port authorities were aroused by the fact that although the ship was offered for sale, steam was always kept up, ready for immediate departure, and that neither the captain nor the crew ever went on shore. An investigation of Lloyds Register of Shipping showed that there was no ship named the *India* answering to the description of the vessel. On April 27th, 1881, the port authorities seized the ship, and it was soon discovered that the *India* was none other than the long-lost *Ferret*. Meanwhile, Mr and Mrs Smith and the captain made good their escape, taking with them a very considerable sum of money, which was never recovered. Smith was arrested a few days later, but for the moment Captain Wright eluded the police. He was eventually brought into court under an assumed name, on a charge of drunkenness and assault. There his identity was discovered, and he was at once re-arrested.

At the subsequent court proceedings, the whole story came to light. Smith was a notorious swindler, well known to the English police. Captain Wright and Walker, the purser, were his confederates. To gain possession of the *Ferret*, Smith opened an account in his own name at one of the leading London banks, and founded the fictitious firm of Henderson & Co, shipbrokers. The balance at the bank was withdrawn a day or so before the ship sailed from Cardiff. The remainder of the ship's company were honest, and completely ignorant of the enterprise. Once at sea, they were intimidated by threats, and promises of large rewards, from disclosing the real state of affairs. At the ports of call, only Smith and Walker went on shore. Captain Wright never left the ship.

After the ship had passed Gibraltar in the previous November, her appearance was altered, and the name changed to *Bentan*. Some wreckage was jettisoned to give the impression of total loss, and the captain set out for the Atlantic, passing Gibraltar unnoticed, under cover of darkness. After calling at the Cape Verde Islands for water and stores, the ship reached the Brazilian port of Santos early in January 1881. By means of forged documents, a valuable cargo of coffee was secured, and the *Bentan* put to sea once more, ostensibly bound for Marseilles. Once out of sight of land she headed south, and in due course reached Cape Town. On the voyage the name was again changed, to *India*. The stolen cargo was disposed of at a handsome figure, but an attempt to sell the ship failed. When the negotiations fell through, the *India* hurriedly left port, and headed towards the Southern Ocean. On arrival in Melbourne, the whole plot was discovered.

By no means the least remarkable part of the whole affair was the verdict of the Australian court. No account was taken of the series of frauds in English and foreign ports, and Smith, Walker and Wright were found not guilty on the charge of attempting to steal the *Ferret*. On the other hand, they were convicted of conspiracy to defraud the intending purchasers of the vessel in Melbourne, and of conspiracy to deceive the Customs and Trade Commissioner by changing the name of the ship. Smith and Walker were sentenced to seven years' penal servitude, and Wright to three and a half years. The rest of the crew were discharged.

At the conclusion of the trial the ship was restored to her rightful owners. The Highland Railway's agent in Australia was authorized to sell her, and the *Ferret* passed to the Adelaide Steam Ship Co. She was eventually wrecked on the Yorke Peninsula, South Australia, in November 1920.

END OF MARITIME ACTIVITIES

The *Carham* remained at Strome Ferry for a short time after the withdrawal of the *Ferret*, but the railway Company withdrew in favour of MacBrayne in 1880. The daily service to Portree was continued, but for some time the Stornoway ship ran on certain days of the week only. Later on, however, regular daily sailings were introduced. In 1897 the steamers were transferred from Strome Ferry to Kyle of Lochalsh.

After lying idle for some time, the *Carham* was sold in 1883 to the Ramsgate Steam Ship Company and renamed *Queen of*

Thanet. For three seasons she worked a regular service between Ramsgate and the holiday resorts on the French coast. These trips were popularly known as 'Shilling Emetics'. In 1886 the ship was again sold, to a Liverpool owner, and broken up two years later.

The steamer services from Strome Ferry do not represent the whole of the Highland Railway's maritime activities. On April 24th, 1877, the Company was empowered to own and work its own ships, and an order was placed with Gourlay Brothers & Co, of Dundee, for an iron-screw steamer (384 tons gross), the *John o' Groat*. On July 27th following the ship was placed in service between Scrabster Harbour (Thurso) and Kirkwall and Stromness, in Orkney.

Regular sailings continued until the summer of 1882. By that time the Company had given up its west-coast steamers, and was anxious to relinquish remaining shipping interests. At the same time it was unwilling to withdraw the ship until assured that the service would be maintained by some independent concern.

The sailings between Thurso and Orkney were continued by the North of Scotland & Orkney & Shetland Steam Navigation Co. The Highland Railway provided the trains in connexion, but, as at Strome Ferry, made no further attempt to run its own ships.

The *John o' Groat* was sold to foreign owners, and in the course of the next ten years passed through several hands. On December 19th, 1892, while sailing in the Adriatic under the Austrian flag, and renamed *Agathé*, the vessel struck a rock off Ancona, and became a total loss.

CHAPTER THIRTEEN

THE LMS REGIME AND NATIONALIZATION

THE PASSING OF THE HIGHLAND

IT WAS realized that it would be impossible for the railways to revert to their former condition after the cessation of hostilities, and various schemes were produced for complete unification or amalgamations on a large scale. Meanwhile, Government control was maintained. At one stage it was proposed that the Scottish railways should form a single group, independent of any of the English lines. But this scheme was found to be unworkable, because of the relatively weaker financial position of the Scottish companies as compared to the larger English ones. At length, the Railway Companies' Association introduced an alternative scheme, which, with minor amendments, was embodied in the Railways Act of August 19th, 1921.

The Act provided for the formation of four large groups, the Highland Railway being included in the largest of them to become part of the London, Midland & Scottish Railway. The LMSR had a route mileage of 7,500, of which total the Highland Railway's contribution was little more than 500 miles. But the Highland's importance as a constituent company of the amalgamated system was none the less on that account. Highland Railway debentures and stocks were exchanged for equivalent holdings in the new Company, but the shareholders of the Dornoch and Wick & Lybster Light Railways were bought out for cash at valuation. One Highland director, A. E. Pullar, deputy chairman since 1916, was appointed to the new Board. The LMSR came into being on January 1st, 1923.

PRUNING OF BRANCHES

Although the disappearance of much that was characteristic of the Highland Railway was an inevitable sequel of the grouping, there were few sudden breaks with the past. That the changes should have been gradual is not surprising, in view of the highly individualistic nature of the system, and the strong local patriotism of the staff. Most of the innovations were made possible by the greater resources of the new and larger Company. Two particularly welcome improvements were the extended use of corridor coaches, and an increase in the number of trains with a refreshment car for at least part of the journey. Among the first services to benefit were those on the northern main line, to which refreshment cars were introduced in the summer of 1923. These cars worked daily return trips from Inverness to The Mound or Helmsdale and at times to Wick. Since June 14th, 1965, the two cars have worked between Inverness and Thurso. On the Kyle line, working was sometimes throughout and at others to Achnasheen, where the car was transferred to the up train in the crossing loop. A buffet-observation car ran until October 2nd, 1967, but there are now no refreshment facilities on the branch.

A problem which had not been solved when the Highland Railway lost its separate identity was the future of the branch from Keith to Portessie. Goods traffic was working over the $2\frac{1}{2}$ miles from Keith to the distillery at Aultmore, and fish traffic was using the $1\frac{1}{2}$ miles between the Highland station at Buckie and the junction with the Great North of Scotland Railway at Portessie, but the track had been removed from the intervening 10 miles after passenger trains and through goods services had been withdrawn in August 1915.

Some twelve months after the grouping, the dismantled section was relaid, and preparations for re-opening even went so far as changing the name of Drybridge station to Letterfourie. However, a final appraisal of the amount of traffic likely to be carried appears to have been unfavourable, because through working was not resumed. Eventually, fish traffic at the Bannffshire ports declined to such an extent that the Highland station at Buckie was no longer required, and the track was removed throughout the line from Aultmore to the junction at Portessie.

Halts at Balnaguard on the Aberfeldy branch and at Parkside, Roster Road and Welsh's Crossing on the Lybster branch were the only *additions* during the 25 years of grouping. During this period no stations were closed apart from those on branches listed in Appendix III.

As was frequently the case elsewhere, traffic on secondary routes in northern Scotland declined seriously with the development of bus services. The first of the former Highland Railway lines to be affected were the branches from Alves to Burghead and Hopeman, and from Orbliston Junction to Fochabers, from which passenger services were withdrawn on September 14th, 1931. The latter was particularly vulnerable to road competition, because its terminus had been placed some distance from the town, to avoid a costly bridge over the Spey.

On the former Caledonian main line between Perth and Stanley, the two intermediate stations at which certain Highland trains called have not survived; Strathord was closed to passengers on April 13th, 1931, and Luncarty on June 18th, 1951, though the goods depots at both stations continued in use for many years.

Two more branches succumbed during the Second World War. All passenger traffic, except special military trains, ceased on the branch to Fort George on April 5th, 1943, and the Wick & Lybster Light Railway was closed completely on April 1st, 1944, and subsequently dismantled. The improvement of the steeply-graded road over the Ord of Caithness had placed the Lybster line at a serious disadvantage. The distance by road between Lybster and Helmsdale is little more than 20 miles; by rail via Wick it was 74 miles. Less than twelve months after hostilities had ended, the Strathpeffer branch, on which services had been drastically reduced, ceased to carry passengers on February 23rd, 1946.

TRAIN-SERVICE DEVELOPMENTS

The general pattern of the train services remained unchanged after the grouping. Such alterations as did occur generally tended towards improvement and acceleration. Sunday services were restored in the summer of 1929, when one train in each direction began to run between Perth and Inverness, via Forres, in connexion with the night trains to and from the south. From the summer of 1934, a relief train ran from Inverness to Perth, via Carr Bridge, but there was no corresponding service in the opposite direction. In May of that year, Sunday services were resumed on the northern main line with a train from Lairg, reaching Inverness in time to connect with the afternoon departure for Perth. This service was balanced by a morning train from Inverness to Lairg, which connected with a night newspaper train from the south and did not carry passengers.

An outstanding development in 1936 was a new weekday evening train, leaving Perth at 6.5 and reaching Inverness at 9.40. It ran during the summer only, and had through coaches from Glasgow and a connexion from Edinburgh. By leaving Kings Cross at 7.25 AM it was possible to travel from London to Inverness by day, with changes at Edinburgh and Perth.

On the northern main line, the 'Further North Express' was restored in the summer of 1923, in the northbound direction, and on Fridays only. The train started from Aviemore, in connexion with the midday service from Perth, and ran non-stop to Dingwall in 95 m. Passengers from Inverness had to travel by the afternoon stopping train to Helmsdale, and change into the express. This arrangement lasted for one season only; when the train was restored in 1924, it ran to and from Inverness, and once a week in each direction. By the summer of 1933 it was running three days a week. It was then renamed the 'John o'Groat', and became a daily train a year later.

The early-morning train from Inverness to the north, and

the afternoon return service, which connected with the ship plying between Scrabster Harbour (Thurso) and Orkney, were named the 'Orcadian' in 1936. Three years earlier, the trains to and from Kyle of Lochalsh in connexion with MacBrayne's ships had been named the 'Hebridean' and the 'Lewisman' respectively. The practice of naming trains on the lines north of Inverness was not generally resumed after the war, but in 1962 the name 'Orcadian' was again used for the fastest summer train.

On the southern main line the only named service was the night train between London (Euston) and Inverness, which became the 'Royal Highlander' in 1928. September of that year saw the introduction of much-needed third-class sleeping berths on the principal Anglo-Scottish services, including the 'Royal Highlander' and the portion of the train which then ran to and from Kings Cross by the East Coast route. The sleeping-cars run between Glasgow and Inverness remained first class only until new composite vehicles were placed in service in the summer of 1932.

During the Second World War, the railways were again called upon to handle a vast amount of additional traffic. The state of emergency lasted for nearly six years, but, thanks to the relatively greater resources of the LMSR, the strain of the burden in the north of Scotland tended to be less severe than it was on the smaller Highland Railway in the earlier conflict. Train services were reduced and schedules were eased; restaurant-cars and some through coaches were suspended, but inconvenience to passengers was reduced to a minimum. The sleeping-car services were maintained between London and Inverness by the West Coast route, and between Glasgow and Inverness, but the through coaches and sleeping cars between London and the Highlands by the East Coast route were withdrawn, and were not restored.

Recovery after the war was slow, and was by no means complete when the railways were nationalized on January 1st, 1948. With the collective name of British Railways, the system was divided into six regions on a geographical basis, and the railways of Scotland were separated from the lines south of the Border, and placed in the Scottish Region. At the time of its formation the region had a route mileage of rather more than 3,700 to which the surviving lines of the Highland Railway contributed some 480 miles.

FROM STEAM TO DIESEL

Of the 150 Highland Railway locomotives which received LMSR numbers after the grouping, only 29 were still at work in January 1948. All the others had passed to the scrapheap, with the exception of the first of the 'Jones Goods' 4–6–0s, No 103 (LMSR No 17916), which had been partly restored to its original condition and livery, and preserved at the former Caledonian Railway works at St Rollox, Glasgow, after it was withdrawn from service in 1934. It is now at the Glasgow Museum of Transport. The survivors comprised eight 4–6–0s (two of the 'Clan' class, and six of the mixed-traffic class); twelve 4–4–0s (two of the 'Loch' class, and ten of the 'Small Ben' class); seven of Drummond's 0–6–0s; and two 0–4–4 tanks, also designed by Drummond.

Withdrawals continued steadily after nationalization, and at the end of 1952 only 4–4–0 No 2 (BR No 54398), *Ben Alder*, and the two 0–4–4 tank engines Nos 25 and 45 (BR Nos 55051 and 55053) remained in service. *Ben Alder* was withdrawn in 1953, and was stored, at first at Inverness and then at Boat of Garten, pending a decision as to its fate. Eventually it was decided to preserve it, and in 1961 it was removed to a shed in the Glasgow area.

The two small tank engines continued at work, and took alternate turns of duty on the Dornoch branch, a line for which their light axle weights made them particularly suitable. No 55051 was withdrawn in the summer of 1956, but No 55053 was overhauled and repainted soon afterwards, and appeared to have been granted an extended lease of life. However, the end came suddenly and ingloriously, early in 1957, when the axle of the leading pair of driving wheels broke while the engine was hauling a mixed train on the branch. One of the wheels became detached, and careered along the track until it came into violent contact with a lineside gatepost. Fortunately, the train was not derailed and nobody was injured. No 55053 was replaced on the Dornoch line by an 0–6–0 pannier tank engine from the Western Region.

The accompanying table shows the Highland Railway locomotives that passed to the Scottish Region. Nine of these veterans were withdrawn from service before they had been renumbered into British Railways stock.

HR No	LMSR No	BR No	Name	Built	Withdrawn
'Clan' class 4–6–0s					
52	14764	—	Clan Munro	1919	1948
55	14767	54767	Clan Mackinnon	1921	1950
Mixed traffic 4–6–0s					
75	17950	57950	—	1918	1950
76	17951	57951	—	1918	1951
78	17953	57953	—	1918	1948
79	17954	57954	—	1919	1952
80	17955	—	—	1919	1952
81	17956	57956	—	1919	1952
'Loch' class 4–4–0s					
119	14379	54379	Loch Insh	1896	1948
125	14385	54385	Loch Tay	1896	1950
'Small Ben' class 4–4–0s					
1	14397	—	Ben-y-Gloe	1898	1949
2	14398	54398	Ben Alder	1898	1953*
3	14399	54399	Ben Wyvis	1898	1952
5	14401	—	Ben Vrackie	1899	1948
7	14403	—	Ben Attow	1899	1949
8	14404	54404	Ben Clebrig	1899	1950
13	14409	54409	Ben Alisky	1900	1950
14	14410	54410	Ben Dearg	1900	1949
41	14415	54415	Ben Bhac Ard	1906	1948
47	14416	54416	Ben a' Bhuird	1906	1948

*Preserved.

o–6–o *goods*

134	17693	—	—	1900	1949
135	17694	—	—	1900	1950
136	17695	57695	—	1900	1952
138	17697	57697	—	1900	1951
139	17698	57698	—	1900	1951
18	17699	—	—	1902	1949
21	17702	—	—	1902	1949

o–4–4 *tanks*

25	15051	55051	*Strathpeffer**	1905	1956
45	15053	55053	—	1905	1957

*Name removed in 1920.

As the Highland locomotives were withdrawn from service they were replaced by motive power from other constituents of the LMSR, and later by post-grouping types. Many locomotives of the former Caledonian Railway were transferred to the north of Scotland, and these were followed by the ubiquitous class '5' 4–6–0s, and after nationalization by standard British Railways designs. Then came the decision that diesel traction was to replace steam as part of the railway modernization plans, announced in 1955. Diesel locomotives began to appear in the Highlands in the spring of 1958, at first on trial trips, and then on regular passenger and freight duties. By June 1961 steam traction had almost disappeared from northern Scotland.

Two-car multiple-unit diesel trains began to work regularly on the local services between Perth and Blair Atholl in June 1959, and multiple-unit sets of the 'inter-city' type were used for the accelerated service between Inverness and Aberdeen inaugurated in July 1960. The trains ran via Mulben, and were allowed 2½ h. for the 108-mile journey, with four intermediate stops. So encouraging were the results that a year later the service was increased from two to four trains in each direction.

NATIONALIZATION

Few changes of great consequence were made in the north of Scotland during the first 12 years of nationalization. Competition from road transport, assisted by the peculiar topography of the coast north of Inverness, resulted in withdrawal of the Black Isle branch passenger service on October 1st, 1951. Goods traffic ceased from June 13th, 1960, and lifting of the track was completed during January 1963. The Dornoch Light Railway was also closed (entirely) from June 13th; dismantling was completed on June 25th, 1963. The only stations closed to passengers on lines that remained open for traffic, were Mosstowie on March 7th, 1955, and Guay on August 3rd, 1959. Per contra, two formerly unadvertised platforms, Tauchers (near Keith) and Duncraig (on the Kyle of Lochalsh line) were inserted in the public timetables from May 23rd, 1949.

The station at Stanley remained in use for passengers until June 11th, 1956. The platforms were subsequently demolished, and the peculiar layout, by which trains on the Highland line observed right-hand running through the station, was simplified, and restored to the form adopted in 1856 for the opening of the Perth & Dunkeld Railway. Trains from Inverness joined the northbound track at the junction, and almost immediately diverged through a crossover to reach the southbound line. A further change took place on September 4th, 1967, when the former Caledonian main line to Forfar was converted to single track and the Highland officially became the 'main line'.

By far the greatest changes since nationalization have occurred on the main line between Inverness and Wick. Including the private station at Dunrobin, this circuitous route had no less than 40 intermediate stations or platforms, some of which were inconveniently situated, and served only small and scattered communities. The main road from Inverness to the north runs roughly parallel with the railway, and in recent years these small stations had lost nearly all their traffic to Highland Omnibuses Limited (a company owned by the then British Transport Commission).

On June 13th, 1960, passenger services were withdrawn from all the intermediate stations between Inverness and Bonar Bridge, except Dingwall, Invergordon, Fearn, and Tain. Beyond Bonar Bridge, bus services do not parallel the railway to the same extent, and on the northern part of the line only the stations at Rogart, The Mound, Loth, Halkirk, Bower, Watten, and Bilbster were closed. The elimination of 20 stops permitted a substantial saving in journey time between Inverness and Wick*. That these economies had been rather too drastic became evident in March 1961, when Rogart station was re-opened as a halt.

Also closed on June 13th, 1960, was the isolated roadside station of Auldearn, some two miles east of Nairn. The original main line of the Highland Railway runs through Nairnshire for about 8 miles and is the only railway in that county. For nearly 40 years after the station at Cawdor was closed in 1858, Nairn was the only station on this section of line, and therefore in the county. Auldearn was opened in 1895, and with its closure, 65 years later, Nairn reverted to its unique position.

The most extensive civil engineering works undertaken in the north of Scotland since nationalization have been the reconstruction of 1 mile 62 chains of the Kyle of Lochalsh line, to enable the level of Lochluichart to be raised in connexion with a hydro-electric project. The works included a new bridge of 100-ft span over the River Conon, the formation of rock cuttings and stone-pitched embankments, and the re-siting of Lochluichart station. The new line (only 43 yards longer than the old) was brought into use on May 3rd, 1954.

THE CENTENARY AND THE FUTURE

A noteworthy post-war development on the southern main line was the restoration, in the autumn of 1955, of the evening train from Perth to Inverness, which now runs throughout the year, and not during the summer only. At first, this train had good connexions from southern Scotland, and the north of England, but passengers from London had to leave King's Cross before 4 AM. Two years later, the morning 'Talisman' was inaugu-

* The financial saving was £41,000 per year.

rated, and the departure time from King's Cross became
7.45 AM, but there was an interval of nearly 1½ h. between the
arrival of the new express in Edinburgh and the departure of
the connexion for Perth and Inverness.

It was not until the summer of 1962 that the acceleration to
a six-hour schedule of the 'Elizabethan' between London and
Edinburgh gave a departure at 9.30 AM and an arrival at 9.25
PM in Inverness, with 33 m. for changing trains in Edinburgh.
In the winter service, a further improvement has enabled an
Inverness connexion to be given from the 10 AM train from
King's Cross.

Journeys to and from the Highlands at weekends were
facilitated in the autumn of 1957, when for the first time the
sleeping-cars and through coaches leaving London (Euston)
for Perth on Saturday evenings were extended to Inverness,
via Forres, on Sunday mornings. Not only was a change of
train, and a long wait, at Perth eliminated, but arrival times at
stations on the Highland line became considerably earlier. A
corresponding southbound train left Inverness on Sunday
evenings. From the summer of 1959 a sleeping-car ran between
Edinburgh and Inverness, in addition to the car to and from
Glasgow.

The table on pages 202–4 shows a summary of services
on the main lines from Perth to Inverness and from Inverness
to the north at salient dates from the autumn of 1863, when the
route through the Central Highlands was opened. At that time,
the northern line extended no farther than Invergordon, but
the figures for 1874 show it open to Wick. The substantial
improvements of the summer of 1885 appear in the third
section of the table, and the effects of the opening of the
shortened route to Inverness in the fourth. The times for
August 1914 and August 1939 show the position immediately
before the outbreak of the two world wars, and those for 1922
and 1947 the services on the eve of the grouping and nationalization respectively. The accelerations that have followed the
introduction of diesel traction are apparent from the times
shown for the summers of 1962 and 1971.

In every case, only trains making the through journey are shown in the summaries, and except for the 'Further North Express' (in the table for August 1914) trains running only on certain days of the week have been omitted. After 1898, trains shown running via Forres have been included only because they did not also serve the Carr Bridge lines.

The centenary year (1963) of the opening of the main line from Forres to Perth across the Grampians, passed without further closures, but 1964 saw the local passenger service between Keith Junction and Elgin via Mulben withdrawn and the disappearance from the timetable of a few wayside stations. The Aberfeldy branch ceased to carry passengers in May 1965, only two months short of its centenary, and the old main line between Forres and Aviemore closed to all traffic in October, thus reducing the route mileage of the former Highland Railway by some 103 miles.

The remodelling of the junction at Stanley was only one of a number of signalling and track layout changes which had started after the end of the Second World War. They were, of course, made in the interests of economy – especially of man-power – and were the precursors of intensified rationalization to follow. This consisted of closure of many signal boxes (in Highland days officially called 'cabins') on both double and single line sections, replacement of two boxes by a single one at larger stations, such as Ballinluig, Blair Atholl, Aviemore and Grantown-on-Spey West, and closure of crossing loops. It should be pointed out that at many wayside stations, particularly north of Inverness, the electric tablet instruments were placed in the station offices, the two 'signal boxes' required to control the North and South loop points and relevant signals being, in effect, only unmanned ground frames. It was not uncommon to see the porter-signalman or stationmaster, cycling along the platform to set the road for the passing of a train. Tablets were exchanged at most boxes by automatic apparatus, but hand exchange was also in force, especially where the instruments were located in the office. At the time of writing (July 1971) the longest single line section is between Helmsdale and Forsinard, 24 miles 24 chains. Details of these changes appear in the notes to the Distance Tables, Appendix II.

As part of the rationalization programme, several double line sections were singled and worked at first by electric token system, replaced on the southern main line line by the tokenless block system in 1968–71 (see Appendix V). On minor branches still worked by electric tablet, this was withdrawn and 'one engine' working substituted.

Further economies have been made by de-staffing of level crossings or providing alternative means of protecting the crossing where there is no longer a signal box from which the gates were formerly worked. In 1966–67 those at Kinloss, Brodie, Gollanfield and Dalcross were equipped with automatic half-barriers actuated by approaching trains. North and West of Inverness, where neither rail nor road traffic justifies such expense, there are now 12 open crossings, without gates or barriers, safety being secured either by automatic red and green traffic lights to control road traffic, or a severe speed restriction on passing trains; in some cases the train is brought to a stand and the engine horn sounded before passing over the roadway.

Though the outlook for the railways in Northern Scotland is uncertain, efforts towards halting the depopulation of the northern counties by introducing industrial development are going ahead and meeting with some success. The effects of the complex at Invergordon are being felt and these will, no doubt, continue.

On the passenger side, whilst the main line south of Inverness and the greatly-improved Aberdeen–Inverness services are not in immediate danger, the same cannot be said of the northern lines. Both the Inverness, Wick & Thurso and Kyle of Lochalsh services are grant-aided under section 39 of the Transport Act 1968, the former receiving £584,000 for 1970–72 and the latter £179,000 for 1970–71. At present three passenger trains are run in each direction over the full length of each line. British Railways have given notice of intention to withdraw the Kyle services in October 1971 but the outcome is not yet known.

AUTHORIZATION AND OPENING DATES

Line	Authorized	Opened to public traffic
Stanley Junction to Dunkeld ...	July 10th, 1854	April 7th, 1856
Inverness to Nairn	July 24th, 1854	Nov 6th, 1855
Inverness Harbour Branch ...	July 24th, 1854	Nov 6th, 1855
Nairn to Dalvey (a)	July 21st, 1856	Dec 22nd, 1857
Dalvey to Elgin	July 21st, 1856	March 25th, 1858
Elgin to Keith	July 21st, 1856	Aug 18th, 1858
Kinloss to Findhorn (b) ...	April 19th, 1859	April 18th, 1860
Inverness to Dingwall ...	July 3rd, 1860	June 11th, 1862
Dingwall to Invergordon ...	July 3rd, 1860	March 25th, 1863
Alves to Burghead (c)	May 17th, 1861	Dec 22nd, 1862
Dunkeld to Pitlochry	July 22nd, 1861	June 1st, 1863
Forres to Aviemore	July 22nd, 1861	Aug 3rd, 1863
Aviemore to Pitlochry ...	July 22nd, 1861	Sept 9th, 1863
Ballinluig to Aberfeldy ...	July 22nd, 1861	July 3rd, 1865
Invergordon to Meikle Ferry (d)	May 11th, 1863	June 1st, 1864
Meikle Ferry to Bonar Bridge	May 11th, 1863	Oct 1st, 1864
Bonar Bridge to Golspie (e) ...	June 29th, 1865	April 13th, 1868
Dingwall to Strome Ferry (f)	July 5th, 1865	Aug 19th, 1870
Golspie to Helmsdale (g) ...	June 20th, 1870	June 19th, 1871
Helmsdate to Wick	July 13th, 1871	July 28th, 1874
Georgemas to Thurso	July 13th, 1871	July 28th, 1874
Canal Junction to Muirtown Basin (h)	July 4th, 1890	April 9th, 1877
Keith to Portessi (i)	July 12th, 1882	Aug 1st, 1884
Fodderty Junction to Strathpeffer	July 28th, 1884	June 3rd, 1885
Aviemore to Carr Bridge ...	July 28th, 1884	July 8th, 1892
Carr Bridge to Daviot ...	July 28th, 1884	July 19th, 1897
Daviot to Millburn Junction ...	July 28th, 1884	Nov 1st, 1898
Burghead to Hopeman ...	July 4th, 1890	Oct 10, 1892
Muir of Ord to Fortrose (j) ...	July 4th, 1890	Feb 1st, 1894
Gollanfield Junction to Fort George	July 4th, 1890	July 1st, 1899

Orbliston Junction to Fochabers	June 27th, 1892	Oct 16th, 1893
Strome Ferry to Kyle of Lochalsh	June 29th, 1893	Nov 2nd, 1897
The Mound to Dornoch (*k*) ...	Aug 13th, 1898	June 2nd, 1902
Wick to Lybster (*k*)	Nov 27th, 1899	July 1st, 1903

(*a*) Temporary station, near Forres, closed when the Findhorn Viaduct was completed, and the line opened to Elgin.

(*b*) Regular services withdrawn on January 1st, 1869. The rails were subsequently removed.

(*c*) Old terminus on Burghead Pier, subsequently the goods station.

(*d*) Temporary station, 4 miles west of Tain, closed in 1869.

(*e*) Sutherland Railway: authorized from Bonar Bridge to Brora, but only completed to Golspie.

(*f*) Dingwall & Skye Railway: authorized from Dingwall to Kyle of Lochalsh, but only completed to Strome Ferry, opened for goods traffic August 5th, 1870.

(*g*) The Duke of Sutherland's Railway. Opened from Dunrobin to West Helmsdale on November 1st, 1870.

(*h*) The line was constructed without Parliamentary powers. In 1890 it was deemed advisable to obtain official sanction.

(*i*) Line closed to passengers on August 9th, 1915.

(*j*) Railway authorized from Muir of Ord to Rosemarkie, but completed to Fortrose only.

(*k*) Authorized under Light Railways Act of 1896, and nominally independent until the grouping.

DISTANCE TABLES

Distances as at September 1925 with subsequent amendments and additions. All stations on single lines have crossing loops except where otherwise shewn.

Perth to Inverness, direct via Carr Bridge

	Mls	Chs	See note
PERTH	0	00	
Luncarty	4	16	1
Strathord	5	12	1
Stanley	7	18	
Murthly	10	28	
Kingswood Crossing	12	71	2
Dunkeld & Birnam	15	45	
Inchmagranachan Crossing	17	77	3
Dalguise	20	23	4
Guay	21	36	5
Ballinluig	23	44	6
Moulinearn Crossing	25	62	7
Pitlochry	28	36	
Killiecrankie	32	16	8
BLAIR ATHOLL	35	20	9

Blair Atholl to Dalwhinnie singled July 11th, 1966

	Mls	Chs	See note
Black Island Platform	36	16	10
Struan	39	65	11
Dalanraoch	44	49	12
Edendon box	48	00	13
Dalnaspidal	50	79	
Druimuachdar Summit	53	00	
Balsporran box	54	69	14
Dalwhinnie	58	48	
Inchlea Crossing	62	44	15
Etteridge Crossing	65	72	16
Newtonmore	68	58	
Kingussie	71	48	
Balavil box	74	18	17

Kincraig	77	33	18
Dalraddy Crossing	79	49	19
AVIEMORE	83	26	20
Carr Bridge	90	02	21
Slochd Crossing	95	29	22
Tomatin	98	79	23
Moy	103	10	24
Daviot	107	04	25

Daviot to Culloden Moor singled March 31st, 1968

Culloden Moor	111	27	
INVERNESS –			
Millburn box	117	34	26
Welsh's Bridge box	117	50	
Locomotive box	117	62	
Station	117	78	

1 Boxes closed July 30th, 1961; **2** Box and loop opened June 3rd, 1908, closed December 15th, 1963; **3** Box and loop opened July 8th, 1897, closed August 24th, 1947; **4** Box and loop closed August 23rd, 1964; **5** No loop; **6** South box closed and line singled between South and North boxes November 12th, 1967, latter renamed 'Ballinluig'; **7** Box and loop opened July 8th, 1897, closed August 31st, 1947; **8** Loop opened July 9th, 1896, box and loop closed December 22nd, 1963; **9** North box closed and line singled between South and North boxes August 25th, 1968, South box renamed 'Blair Atholl'; **10** Not advertised, closed April 11th, 1959; **11** box closed July 13th, 1965; **12** Old box (double line) closed and replaced by new box and loop at 45 m 61 ch July 11th, 1966; **13** (double line) Box closed December 16th, 1951; **14** Opened June 1st, 1908, reopened on new site October 25th, 1942, closed December 16th, 1951, then opened as required for summer traffic and finally closed October 28th, 1963; **15** Old box and loop opened July 8th, 1897, replaced by new box 9 ch further north, box and loop closed January 11th, 1966; **16** Box and loop opened June 25th, 1911, closed May 7th, 1963; **17** Box opened December, 1942, closed August 31st, 1947; **18** Box and loop closed January 10th, 1966; **19** Box and loop opened June 28th, 1903, closed September 14th, 1937, reopened December 20th, 1942, closed August 24th, 1947; **20** South and North boxes closed and replaced by new box ('Aviemore') 83 m 46 ch, line through station singled and converted to crossing loop April 4th, 1971; **21** South and North boxes closed and replaced by new box on up platform December 15th, 1957; **22** New box 95 m 33 ch replacing former South box (which housed the token instruments), opened July 23rd, 1944. Box and loop closed December 15th, 1963; **23** South and North boxes closed and replaced by new box ('Tomatin') August 11th, 1968; **24** South and North boxes and loop closed December 15th, 1963; **25** Box and loop closed December 14th, 1969; **26** Mileage of old box, new box 117 m 18 ch.

Aviemore and Keith to Inverness

	from Perth		from Keith		See
	Mls	Chs	Mls	Chs	note
AVIEMORE	83	26			
Boat of Garten	88	40			1
Broomhill	92	55			2
Grantown-on-Spey	95	76			3
Castle Grant Platform	98	21			4
Dava Summit	101	46			
Dava	104	32			5
Dunphail	110	58			5
Dallas Dhu Siding	117	64			
KEITH JUNCTION			0	00	6
Tauchers Platform			3	70	7
Mulben			4	75	8
Orton			8	27	9
Orbliston Junction			11	61	10
Lhanbryde			14	54	2
ELGIN			18	05	11
Mosstowie			21	24	12
Alves			23	21	13
Kinloss			27	08	14
FORRES	119	24	30	20	15
Brodie	122	55	33	51	16
Auldearn	126	31	37	27	17
Nairn	128	63	39	59	
Gollanfield Junction	134	28	45	24	18
Dalcross	137	10	48	06	19

Dalcross to Millburn singled March 12th, 1967

Castle Stuart Platform	138	23	49	19	4
Allanfearn	140	46	51	42	20
INVERNESS –					
Millburn box	143	31	54	27	
Welsh's Bridge box	143	47	54	43	
Locomotive box	143	59	54	55	
Station	143	75	54	71	

1 South and North boxes closed, double line between them singled and made through section Aviemore–Grantown-on-Spey (GNS) station December 6th, 1965; **2** No loop; **3** South and North boxes

closed and replaced by one new box November 23rd, 1952, and this
closed October 18th, 1965; **4** Private station; **5** Boxes closed October
18th, 1965; **6** East and West boxes closed October 23rd, 1966, and
line singled; **7** No loop, platform not advertised until May 23rd,
1949; **8** East and West boxes and loop closed January 19th, 1965;
9 East and West boxes and loop closed January 1947; **10** East and
West boxes and loop closed June 12th, 1966; **11** New West box
6½ chs nearer Inverness opened April 30th, 1951, double line Elgin
Centre box (GNS) to West box; **12** Box and loop (opened July 1st,
1902) closed October 31st, 1948; **13** East and West boxes and loop
closed December 11th, 1966, and junction with Burghead branch
controlled by a ground frame; **14** East and West boxes and loop
(opened May 30th, 1904) closed November 6th, 1966; **15** South box
closed August 15th, 1966, West box closed and line singled between
East and West boxes and new loop provided at East box (renamed
'Forres') May 28th, 1967; **16** East and West boxes and loop closed
May 8th, 1966; **17** Box and loop (opened July 3rd, 1905) closed
June 5th, 1960; **18** Junction and East boxes replaced by new Junction
box to east and loop (opened July 1st, 1899) closed January 16th, 1966;
19 Box closed March 12th, 1967; **20** Box closed October 19th, 1965.

Inverness to Wick and Thurso

	from Perth via Carr Bridge and Inverness station		from Perth via Carr Bridge and Inverness Loop		See note
	Mls	Chs	Mls	Chs	
INVERNESS –					
Millburn box	117	34	117	34	
Welsh's Bridge box	117	50	117	50	
Locomotive box	117	62	—		
Station	117	78	—		
Rose Street box	118	28	117	72	
Ness Viaduct box	118	41	118	05	1
Clachnaharry box	119	55	119	19	
Clachnaharry station	119	61	119	25	1
Bruichnain box	120	58			2

Clachnaharry box to Clunes singled May 2nd, 1966

Bunchrew	121	34			3
Lentran	123	45			4
Clunes	125	29			5
Beauly	127	67			6
Muir of Ord	130	61			

			Mls	Chs	
Conon	133	78			7
DINGWALL	136	34			8
Foulis	140	51			9
Evanton	142	58			10
Alness	146	25			11
INVERGORDON	149	12			
Delny	152	53			12
Kildary	154	35			13
Nigg	156	79			12
Fearn	158	34			14
TAIN	162	00			
Glenmorangie Siding	163	19			15
Edderton	167	29			16
Mid Fearn Halt	172	78			17
Bonar Bridge	175	43			
Culrain	178	51			18
Invershin	179	07			12
Lairg	184	49			
Lairg Summit	187	05			
Acheildh Crossing	190	22			19
Rogart	194	47			
The Mound	198	44			20
GOLSPIE	202	06			21
Dunrobin (Private)	203	72			12
Brora	208	15			
Loth	213	39			12
Helmsdale	219	10			
Salzcraggie Platform	221	70			12
Kildonan	228	52			22
Borrobol Platform	232	42			12
Kinbrace	235	71			22
Forsinard	243	34			
County March Summit	247	39			
Altnabreac	251	56			23
Scotscalder	260	61			24
Halkirk	263	39			12
Georgemas	264	79	0	00	
Hoy			0	75	12
THURSO			6	52	25
Bower	267	59			12
Watten	271	50			22
Bilbster	274	07			12
WICK	279	14			

1 Closed; 2 Box and loop opened March 15th, 1902, became part of double line between Clachnaharry and Bunchrew opened June 23rd, 1913; 3 Box closed May 2nd, 1966; 4 Loop opened May 2nd,1966; 5 Loop opened June 13th, 1904, subsequently formed the end of the doubling from Clachnaharry opened June 1st, 1914, box closed May 2nd, 1966; 6 South and North boxes and loop closed July 20th, 1965; 7 Box and loop (opened June 29th, 1911) closed November 22nd, 1961; 8 New North box 130 yards north of former box opened November 3rd, 1963; 9 Box and loop (opened October 4th, 1916, located south of station) closed July 24th, 1949; 10 South and North boxes and loop closed June 7th, 1962; 11 South and North boxes and loop closed January 15th, 1967; 12 No loop; 13 South and North boxes and loop closed July 26th, 1965; 14 Box and loop (opened July 30th, 1910) closed October 9th, 1966, replaced by ground frame to control siding points; 15 Closed June 1970; 16 South and North boxes and loop closed April 10th, 1962; 17 Closed to public traffic September 1st, 1865, then unadvertised; 18 Box and loop opened June 2nd, 1902, closed May 8th, 1962; 19 Opened July 1st, 1909, closed November 11th, 1956; 20 Box and loop (goods trains only) closed June 25th, 1963; 21 South and North boxes and loop closed October 2nd, 1966, replaced by ground frame to control siding points; 22 South and North boxes and loop closed November 20th, 1966; 23 South and North boxes and loop closed September 25th, 1966; 24 South and North boxes and loop closed November 17th, 1964; 25 Box closed August 9th, 1970, and branch converted to 'one train' working.

Dingwall to Kyle of Lochalsh and Strathpeffer

	from Perth via Carr Bridge				See
	Mls	Chs	Mls	Chs	note
DINGWALL	136	34			
Fodderty Junction	138	56	138	56	1
Strathpeffer			141	14	
Achterneed	141	07			2
Garve	148	23			
Lochluichart (new station)*	153	44			3
Achanalt	157	74			4
Achnasheen	164	24			
Loan Crossing	170	44			5

*Distances from Lochluichart onwards as amended from May 3rd, 1954.

Glencarron	172	52	3
Achnashellach	176	66	6
Strathcarron	182	23	
Attadale	184	49	3
Stromeferry	189	42	7
Duncraig	193	36	8
Plockton	194	49	3
Duirinish	196	03	9
KYLE OF LOCHALSH	200	06	

1 Box closed 1936, reopened June 23rd, 1940, closed August 20th, 1944; 2 Box and loop closed March 24th, 1966; 3 No loop; 4 East and West boxes and loop closed March 23rd, 1966; 5 Opened February 1st, 1918, closed 1920, removed by 1922; 6 Box and loop (opened June 1st, 1900) closed March 22nd, 1966; 7 East and West boxes and loop closed March 20th, 1966; 8 Formerly private platform, made public from May 23rd, 1949; 9 No loop but box opened April 28th, 1940, closed October 28th, 1945.

Aberfeldy branch

	Mls	Chs	
Ballinluig	0	00	
Balnaguard Halt	2	11	no loop
Grandtully	4	27	no loop
Aberfeldy	8	59	

Black Isle branch

	Mls	Chs	
Muir of Ord	0	00	
Redcastle	3	58	no loop
Allangrange	5	39	no loop
Munlochy	8	02	no loop
Avoch	11	25	no loop
Fortrose	13	45	

Dornoch Light Railway

	Mls	Chs	
The Mound	0	00	
Cambusavie Halt	1	28	no loop
Skelbo	3	60	no loop
Embo	5	33	no loop
Dornoch Level Crossing	7	31	
Dornoch	7	51	

Wick & Lybster Light Railway

	Mls	Chs	
Wick	0	00	
Wick Junction	0	19	
Thrumster	4	32	no loop
Welsh's Crossing Halt	6	52	
Ulbster	7	47	no loop
Mid Clyth	9	52	no loop
Roster Road Halt	10	09	
Occumster	12	32	no loop
Parkside Halt	12	72	
Plantation Level Crossing	13	26	
Lybster	13	63	

Portessie branch

	Mls	Chs	
Keith station	0	00	
Keith Junction West	0	18	
Aultmore	2	37	no loop
Enzie	7	63	no loop
Drybridge Platform	10	03	no loop
Rathven	11	29	no loop
Buckie	12	26	
Portessie	13	64	
Junction with GNSR	13	71	

Fochabers branch

	Mls	Chs	
Orbliston Junction	0	00	
Balnacoul Halt	2	19	no loop
Fochabers Town	3	00	

Hopeman branch

	Mls	Chs	
Alves	0	00	
Coltfield Platform	2	20	no loop
Burghead	5	05	
Burghead Old Station	5	37	known as 'Harbour Extension'
Hopeman	7	05	

Fort George branch

	Mls	Chs
Gollanfield Junction	0	00
Fort George	1	38

Invergarry & Fort Augustus Railway
(worked by the Highland Railway 1903 to 1907)

	Mls	Chs
Spean Bridge	0	00
Gairlochy	2	58
Invergloy Platform	7	29
Invergarry	15	12
Aberchalder	19	34
Fort Augustus	23	19
Fort Augustus Pier	24	16

CLOSURES

Line	Miles	Closed to passengers	Closed entirely
Inverness Harbour branch	¾	June 1867	
Kinloss to Findhorn	3	Jan 1st, 1869	c. 1880
Burghead to Burghead Harbour[1]	½	Oct 10th, 1892	Nov 7th, 1966
Keith to Aultmore	2½	Aug 9th, 1915	Oct 3rd, 1966
Aultmore to Buckie	9¾	Aug 9th, 1915	Aug 9th, 1915
Buckie to Portessie	1½	Aug 9th, 1915	April 1st, 1944
Alves to Burghead	5½	Sept 14th, 1931	
Burghead to Hopeman	2	Sept 14th, 1931	Dec 31st, 1957
Orbliston Junction to Fochabers Town	3	Sept 14th, 1931	March 28th, 1966[2]
Gollanfield Junction to Fort George	1½	April 5th, 1943	Aug 11th, 1958[3]
Wick to Lybster	13¾	April 1st, 1944	April 1st, 1944
Fodderty Junction to Strathpeffer	2½	Feb 23rd, 1946	March 26th, 1951[4]
Muir of Ord to Fortrose	13½	Oct 1st, 1951	June 13th, 1960
The Mound to Dornoch	7¾	June 13th, 1960	June 13th, 1960
Keith Junction to Elgin (via Mulben)[5]	18	Dec 18th, 1964	
Ballinluig to Aberfeldy	8¾	May 3rd, 1965	Jan 25th, 1965
Dallas Dhu Siding to Forres East	1¾	Oct 18th, 1965	May 21st, 1967[6]
Aviemore to Boat of Garten	5¼	Oct 18th, 1965	June 16th, 1969
Boat of Garten to Dallas Dhu Siding	29¼	Oct 18th, 1965	Oct 18th, 1965
Forres West Curve	¼	Oct 18th, 1965	Aug 15th, 1966
Invergordon Harbour branch	¼	—	May 31st, 1971

1 Including Burghead first station; 2 Cessation of traffic, officially closed June 12th, 1966; 3 Cessation of traffic, officially closed December 28th, 1961; 4 Cessation of traffic, officially closed August 12th, 1951; 5 Local passenger service only withdrawn and intermediate stations closed; 6 Cessation of traffic, officially closed June 30th, 1967.

Station	Closed to passengers	Closed to goods
Aberfeldy	May 3rd, 1965	Jan 25th, 1965
Achanalt	—	Nov 2nd, 1964
Achnashellach	—	Jan 27th, 1964
Achterneed[1]	Dec 7th, 1964	May 18th, 1964
Allanfearn[2]	May 3rd, 1965	Jan 27th, 1964
Allangrange	Oct 1st, 1951	June 13th, 1960
Alness	June 13th, 1960	—
Altnabreac	—	Aug 15th, 1966
Alves	May 3rd, 1965	Nov 7th, 1966
Attadale	—	Aug 15th, 1966
Auldearn	June 6th, 1960	Sept 7th, 1964
Aultmore[3]	Aug 9th, 1915	Oct 3rd, 1966
Avoch	Oct 1st, 1951	June 13th, 1960
Ballinluig	May 3rd, 1965	
Balnacoul Halt	Sept 14th, 1931	—
Balnaguard[4]	May 3rd, 1965	
Beauly	June 13th, 1960	Jan 25th, 1965
Bilbster	June 13th, 1960	June 13th, 1960
Black Island Platform[5]	April 11th, 1959	
Blair Atholl[6]	—	Nov 7th, 1966
Boat of Garten	Oct 18th, 1965	Nov 2nd, 1964
Borrobol	Nov 29th, 1965	June 15th, 1964
Bower	June 13th, 1960	May 18th, 1964
Brodie	May 3rd, 1965	Dec 28th, 1964
Broomhill	Oct 18th, 1965	Jan 25th, 1965
Buckie	Aug 9th, 1915	Aug 9th, 1915
Bunchrew	June 13th, 1960	Jan 27th, 1964
Burghead (1st station)	Oct 10th, 1892	—
Burghead (2nd station)	Sept 14th, 1931	Nov 7th, 1966*
Cambusavie Halt	June 13th, 1960	
Carr Bridge		Feb 27th, 1967*
Clachnaharry	April 1st, 1913	
Clunes	June 13th, 1960	Jan 27th, 1964
Coltfield Platform[7]	Sept 14th, 1931	—
Conon	June 13th, 1960	Oct 11th, 1965

[1] Opened as Strathpeffer, renamed June 1st, 1865.
[2] Opened as Culloden, renamed November 1st, 1898.
[3] Opened as Forgie, renamed January 1st, 1899.
[4] Opened by LMS Railway December 2nd, 1935.
[5] Not advertised.
[6] Opened as Blair Athole, renamed September 7th, 1893.
[7] Opened as Wards, renamed 1865.
* Except private siding.

Station	Closed to passengers	Closed to goods
Culloden Moor	May 3rd, 1965	Feb 27th, 1967*
Culrain	—	May 18th, 1964
Cummingston	April 1st, 1904	April 1st, 1904
Dalcross	May 3rd, 1965	June 15th, 1964
Dalguise	May 3rd, 1965	Jan 27th, 1964
Dalnaspidal	May 3rd, 1965	Jan 27th, 1964
Dalvey[1]	March 25th, 1858	—
Dalwhinnie	—	Feb 27th, 1967*
Dava	Oct 18th, 1965	Jan 27th, 1964
Daviot	May 3rd, 1965	Sept 7th, 1964
Delny	June 13th, 1960	June 15th, 1964
Dornoch	June 13th, 1960	June 13th, 1960
Drybridge Platform	Aug 9th, 1915	—
Duirinish	—	Feb 1st, 1954
Duncraig[2]	Dec 7th, 1964	—
Dunkeld & Birnam	—	Aug 4th, 1969
Dunphail	Oct 18th, 1965	Nov 2nd, 1964
Dunrobin (Private)[3]	Nov 29th, 1965	Nov 2nd, 1964
Edderton	June 13th, 1960	Nov 2nd, 1964*
Embo	June 13th, 1960	June 13th, 1960
Enzie	Aug 9th, 1915	Aug 9th, 1915
Evanton[4]	June 13th, 1960	Nov 2nd, 1964
Findhorn	Jan 1st, 1869	c. 1880
Fochabers Town[5]	Sept 14th, 1931	March 28th, 1966
Forsinard	—	June 15th, 1964
Fort Augustus Pier	Oct 1st, 1906	July 1924[6]
Fort George	April 5th, 1943	Aug 11th, 1958
Fortrose	Oct 1st, 1951	June 13th, 1960
Foulis[7]	June 13th, 1960	June 13th, 1960
Glencarron	Dec 7th, 1964	—
Gollanfield[8]	May 3rd, 1965	Sept 7th, 1964
Grandtully	May 3rd, 1965	Jan 25th, 1965
Grantown-on-Spey West	Oct 18th, 1965	July 5th, 1965
Guay	Aug 3rd, 1959	Aug 3rd, 1959

[1] Inverness & Aberdeen Junction Railway at closure.

[2] Formerly private station made public May 23rd, 1949.

[3] Goods depot public.   [4] Opened as Novar, renamed June 1st, 1937.

[5] Opened as Fochabers, renamed July 1st, 1894.

[6] Approximate date.

[7] Opened as Fowlis, spelling altered March 20th, 1916.

[8] Opened as Fort George, renamed Gollanfield Junction, July 1st, 1899, and Gollanfield, March 1959.

* Except private siding.

Station	Closed to passengers	Closed to goods
Halkirk	June 13th, 1960	March 29th, 1965
Hopeman	Sept 14th, 1931	Dec 30th, 1957
Hoy	Nov 29th, 1965	Nov 29th, 1965
Inverness Harbour	June 1867[1]	—
Invershin	—	Jan 27th, 1964
Kildary[2]	June 13th, 1960	Jan 25th, 1965
Kildonan	—	Nov 2nd, 1964
Kildrummie[3]	Jan 1858[1]	—
Killiecrankie	May 3rd, 1965	Oct 28th, 1963
Kinbrace	—	March 29th, 1965
Kincraig[4]	Oct 18th, 1965	May 18th, 1964
Kingussie	—	Oct 11th, 1965
Kinloss	May 3rd, 1965	Nov 7th, 1966
Lentran	June 13th, 1960	Sept 7th, 1964*
Lhanbryde	Dec 7th, 1964	May 2nd, 1966
Lochluichart (1st station)	May 3rd, 1954	May 3rd, 1954
Lochluichart (2nd station)[5]	—	Jan 27th, 1964
Loth	June 13th, 1960	May 18th, 1964
Luncarty[6]	June 18th, 1951	May 23rd, 1966
Lybster	April 1st, 1944	April 1st, 1944
Meikle Ferry	Jan 1st, 1869	Jan 1st, 1869
Mid Clyth	April 1st, 1944	April 1st, 1944
Mid Fearn[7]	Sept 1st, 1865	Sept 1st, 1865
Mosstowie	March 7th, 1955	Dec 28th, 1964
Moy	May 3rd, 1965	Jan 27th, 1964
Muir of Ord	June 13th, 1960	—
Mulben	Dec 7th, 1964	April 20th, 1964
Munlochy	Oct 1st, 1951	June 13th, 1960
Murthly	May 3rd, 1965	Aug 4th, 1969
Nigg	June 13th, 1960	Dec 28th, 1964
Occumster	April 1st, 1944	April 1st, 1944
Orbliston[8]	Dec 7th, 1964	April 20th, 1964

[1] Last appearance in timetable.
[2] Opened as Parkhill, renamed 1868.
[3] Opened as Cawdor, renamed 1857.
[4] Opened as Boat of Insh, renamed 1871.
[5] Opened by British Railways May 3rd, 1954.
[6] Caledonian Railway station used by Highland passenger trains.
[7] Continued in use unadvertised.
[8] Opened as Fochabers, renamed Orbliston Junction October 16th, 1893, Orbliston September 12th, 1960.
* Except private siding.

Station	Closed to passengers	Closed to goods
Orton	Dec 7th, 1964	April 20th, 1964
Parkside Halt[1]	April 1st, 1944	—
Plockton	—	Sept 7th, 1964
Rafford	May 31st, 1865	May 31st, 1865
Rathven	Aug 9th, 1915	Aug 9th, 1915
Redcastle	Oct 1st, 1951	June 13th, 1960
Rogart[2]	—	May 18th, 1964
Rohallion	Oct 1864[3]	—
Roster Road Halt[1]	April 1st, 1944	—
Salzcraggie	Nov 29th, 1965	—
Scotscalder	—	Jan 27th, 1964
Skelbo	June 13th, 1960	June 13th, 1960
Stanley[4]	June 11th, 1956	Dec 6th, 1965
Strathord[4]	April 13th, 1931	Nov 2nd, 1964
Strathpeffer	Feb 23rd, 1946	March 26th, 1951
Stromeferry	—	June 15th, 1964
Struan	May 3rd, 1965	Jan 27th, 1964
The Mound	June 13th, 1960	Jan 27th, 1964
Thrumster	April 1st, 1944	April 1st, 1944
Tomatin	May 3rd, 1965	—
Ulbster	April 1st, 1944	April 1st, 1944
Watten	June 13th, 1960	June 15th, 1964
Welsh's Crossing Halt	April 1st, 1944	April 1st, 1944
West Helmsdale	June 19th, 1871	—

[1] Opened by LMS Railway January 27th, 1936.

[2] Closed to passengers June 13th, 1960, reopened as unstaffed halt March 6th, 1961.

[3] Last appearance in timetable.

[4] Caledonian Railway station used by Highland passenger trains.

SUMMARY OF TRAIN SERVICES

Date	No of trains		Fastest train		Slowest train	
September 1863						
Perth and Inverness (via Forres, 144 miles)						
	north	2	6 h.		6 h.	50 m.
	south	2	5 h.	55 m.	7 h.	30 m.
Inverness and Invergordon (31¼ miles)						
	north	4	1 h.	25 m.	1 h.	50 m.
	south	4	1 h.	30 m.	1 h.	40 m.
August 1874						
Perth and Inverness (via Forres)						
	north	4	5 h.	15 m.	8 h.	
	south	4	5 h.	15 m.	9 h.	30 m.
Inverness and Wick (161¼ miles)						
	north	2	7 h.	5 m.	7 h.	25 m.
	south	2	7 h.	10 m.	7 h.	30 m.
July 1885						
Perth and Inverness (via Forres)						
	north	5	4 h.		7 h.	20 m.
	south	5	4 h.		9 h.	
Inverness and Wick						
	north	2	6 h.		8 h.	
	south	2	6 h.	30 m.	9 h.	30 m.
November 1898						
Perth and Inverness (via Carr Bridge, 118 miles)						
	north	5	3 h.	15 m.	4 h.	20 m.
	south	5	3 h.	20 m.	4 h.	23 m.
					6 h.	35 m.[1]
Inverness and Wick						
	north	2	6 h.		6 h.	45 m.
	south	2	6 h.	30 m.	6 h.	45 m.

[1] Via Forres.

Date	No of trains	Fastest train	Slowest train

August 1914
Perth and Inverness (via Carr Bridge)

north	9	3 h. 20 m.	4 h. 36 m.
			4 h. 39 m.[1]
south	8	3 h. 16 m.	4 h. 30 m.
			6 h. 15 m.[1]

Inverness and Wick

north	3	5 h. 30 m.[2]	7 h.
		6 h. 10 m.	
south	3	5 h. 11 m.[2]	6 h. 55 m.
		6 h. 40 m.	

December 1922
Perth and Inverness (via Carr Bridge)

north	5	3 h. 35 m.	4 h. 42 m.
south	5	3 h. 16 m.	4 h. 45 m.

Inverness and Wick

north	2	6 h. 30 m.	7 h. 15 m.
south	2	6 h. 50 m.	7 h. 30 m.

August 1939
Perth and Inverness (via Carr Bridge)

north	9	3 h. 25 m.	4 h. 25 m.
			5 h. 38 m.[1]
south	7	3 h. 21 m.	5 h.

Inverness and Wick

north	3	4 h. 49 m.	6 h. 9 m.
south	3	5 h. 10 m.	6 h. 2 m.

December 1947
Perth and Inverness (via Carr Bridge)

north	7	3 h. 22 m.	4 h. 34 m.
south	5	3 h. 8 m.	5 h. 16 m.

Inverness and Wick

north	2	6 h. 1 m.	6 h. 33 m.
south	2	5 h. 53 m.	6 h. 19 m.

[1] Via Forres.
[2] 'Further North Express', Wednesdays and Fridays from Inverness, and Thursdays and Saturdays from Wick.

Date	No of trains		Fastest train	Slowest train

August 1962
Perth and Inverness (via Carr Bridge)

north	8		3 h. 16 m.	3 h. 45 m.
				5 h. 9 m.[1]
south	7		3 h. 18 m.	5 h. 5 m.

Inverness and Wick

north	4		4 h.	5 h. 8 m.
south	3		4 h.	5 h. 6 m.

May 1971
Perth and Inverness

north	4		2 h. 20 m.	3 h. 35 m.
south	5		2 h. 34 m.	5 h.

Inverness and Wick

north	3		4 h. 39 m.	4 h. 50 m.
south	3		4 h. 43 m.	4 h. 49 m.

[1] Via Forres.

SINGLE LINES AND SIGNALLING ARRANGEMENTS

Doubling of single line sections

Between	Opening date
Blair Atholl and Dalnacardoch box	July 2nd, 1900
Dalnacardoch box and Dalnaspidal	May 13th, 1901
Dalnaspidal and Druimuachdar Summit	June 10th, 1901
Druimuachdar Summit and Balsporran box	June 1st, 1908
Balsporran box and Dalwhinnie	May 17th, 1909
Clachnaharry and Bunchrew	June 23rd, 1913
Bunchrew and Clunes	June 1st, 1914

Singling of double line sections

Between	Date
Boat of Garten North box and Boat of Garten South box	Dec. 6th, 1965
Clachnaharry and Clunes	May 2nd, 1966
Blair Atholl and Dalwhinnie	July 11th, 1966
Keith Junction East box and Keith Junction West box	Oct 23rd, 1966
Dalcross and Inverness, Millburn box	March 12th, 1967
Forres East box and Forres West box	May 28th, 1967
Ballinluig North box and Ballinluig South box	Nov 12th, 1967
Daviot and Culloden Moor	March 31st, 1968
Blair Atholl North box and Blair Atholl South box	Aug 25th, 1968
Aviemore North box and Aviemore South box	April 4th, 1971

Replacement of electric token working by Tokenless Block system on the Perth and Inverness main line

Between	Date
Stanley and Murthly	June 8th, 1969
Murthly and Ballinluig	June 1st, 1969
Ballinluig and Blair Atholl	May 11th, 1969
Blair Atholl and Dalnaspidal	April 27th, 1969

Between	Date
Dalnaspidal and Newtonmore	April 20th, 1969
Newtonmore and Aviemore South box	March 9th, 1969
Aviemore South box and Aviemore North box	April 4th, 1971*
Aviemore North box and Tomatin	Nov 10th, 1968
Tomatin and Culloden Moor	Aug 11th, 1968

*On abolition of double line between these boxes.

Seven intermediate signal boxes can be switched out, leaving a similar number to control the 104-mile single line section. Culloden Moor to Inverness remains double line.

PRINCIPAL ALTITUDES ABOVE SEA LEVEL

	Feet		Feet
Druimuachdar Summit	1,484	Carr Bridge station	914
Slochd Summit	1,315	Kingussie station	745
Dalwhinnie station	1,174	Grantown-on-Spey station	737
Dava Summit	1,052	Boat of Garten station	712
Tomatin station	1,029	County March	
Dava station	985	(Sutherland/Caithness)	708
		Lairg Summit	484

OFFICERS

Inverness & Nairn Railway
Merged with the IAJR on May 17th, 1861.

Chairmen:

| | 1854–6 | Cluny Macpherson |
| | 1857–61 | Eneas William Macintosh |

General manager:

| | 1855–61 | Andrew Dougall |

Secretaries:

| | 1854–6 | Messrs G. & P. Anderson (Inverness)* |
| | 1857–61 | Andrew Dougall |

Locomotive superintendent:

| | 1855–61 | William Barclay |

Engineer:

| | 1854–61 | Joseph Mitchell |

Inverness & Aberdeen Junction Railway
Amalgamated to form the Highland Railway on June 29th, 1865.

Chairman:

| | 1856–65 | Alexander Matheson |

General manager:

| | 1856–65 | Andrew Dougall |

Secretary:

| | 1856–65 | Andrew Dougall |

Locomotive superintendent:

| | 1856–65 | William Barclay |

*Secretary and solicitors

Engineers:
1856–63	Joseph Mitchell
1864–5	Joseph Mitchell & Co

Traffic managers:
1860–63	Thomas Mackay
1864–5	William Roberts*

Inverness & Perth Junction Railway
Amalgamated to form the Highland Railway on June 29th, 1865.

Chairman:
1861–5	The Hon T. C. Bruce

General manager:
1861–5	Andrew Dougall

Secretary:
1861–5	Andrew Dougall

Locomotive superintendent:
1861–5	William Barclay

Engineers:
1861–3	Joseph Mitchell
1864–5	Joseph Mitchell & Co

Traffic managers:
1863	Thomas Mackay
1864–5	William Roberts*

Inverness & Ross-shire Railway
Merged with IAJR on June 30th, 1862.

Chairman:
1860–62	Alexander Matheson

General manager:
1860–62	Andrew Dougall

Secretary:
1860–62	Andrew Dougall

*Designated passenger superintendent

Locomotive superintendent:

      1862   William Barclay

Engineer:

      1860–62   Joseph Mitchell

Traffic manager:

      1862   Thomas Mackay

Sutherland Railway
Merged with the HR on July 28th, 1884. The railway was worked by the HR.

Chairman:

      1865–84   The Duke of Sutherland

Secretary:

      1865–84   Andrew Dougall

Engineers:

      1865–7   Joseph Mitchell & Co
      1868–70   William Baxter

Sutherland & Caithness Railway
Merged with the HR on July 28th, 1884. The railway was worked by the HR.

Chairman:

      1871–84   The Duke of Sutherland

Secretary:

      1871–84   Andrew Dougall

Engineer:

      1871–4   Murdoch Patterson

Caithness Railway
Authorized in 1866, but never commenced.

Chairman:

      1866–71   The Earl of Caithness

Dingwall & Skye Railway
Merged with the HR on August 2nd, 1880. The railway was worked by the HR.

Chairman:
1865–80	Alexander Matheson

Secretary:
1865–80	Andrew Dougall

Engineers:
1865–7	Joseph Mitchell & Co
1868–70	Murdoch Patterson

Perth & Dunkeld Railway
Merged with IPJR on February 28th, 1864. The line was worked by the SNER.

Chairman:
1854–64	The Earl of Mansfield

Secretaries:
1854–7	Archibald Reid
1858–9	C. D. Cranstoun
1860–64	Thomas Fyfe

Engineers:
1854–9	J. W. Stewart
1860–64	John Willet

Findhorn Railway
Worked by IAJR from 1862.

Chairmen:
1859–66	Peter Brown
1867–70	James Forbes
1871–81	John Binning

General manager:
1860–62	Alexander Hutchison

Secretary:
1859–81	John D. Davidson

Engineer:
1859–62	Joseph Mitchell

The Highland Railway
Formed by the amalgamation of the IAJR and IPJR on June 29th, 1865.

Chairmen:

1865–84	Alexander Matheson
1885–91	The Hon T. C. Bruce
1892–6	Eneas Macintosh
1897–1900	Sir George MacPherson Grant
1901	J. D. Fletcher
1902–12	William Whitelaw
1913–15	R. M. Wilson
1916	William Whitelaw
1917–22	W. H. Cox

General managers:

1865–96	Andrew Dougall
1897–8	Charles Steel
1899–1910	Thomas Wilson
1911–22	Robert Park

Secretaries:

1865–96	Andrew Dougall
1897–1901	William Gowenlock
1902–10	Robert Park
1911–22	George Cornet

Locomotive superintendents:

1865–9	William Stroudley
1870–96	David Jones
1897–1911	Peter Drummond
1912–15	Fredrick Smith
1915–22	Christopher Cumming
1922 (April to Dec)	
	David Chalmers Urie

Superintendents of the line:

1865–75	William Roberts
1876–90	Thomas Robertson
1891–1900	William Garrow
1901–22	Thomas McEwen*

*Designated traffic manager

Engineers:

1865–9	J. W. Buttle (*a*)
1870–74	Peter Wilson (*b*)
1875–97	Murdoch Patterson (*c*)
1898–1913	William Roberts (*d*)
1914–22	Alexander Newlands (*d*)

(*a*) Designated superintendent of permanent way
(*b*) Designated resident engineer
(*c*) Designated resident engineer until 1893, then chief engineer
(*d*) Designated engineer

INDEX

David & Charles
Railway Series